ENCOURAGING
WORDS
For Difficult Days

1 & 2 PETER AND JUDE

JIM RICHARDS

Auxano
PRESS

ISBN 978-0-9973414-9-2

Published by Auxano Press
Tigerville, South Carolina
www.AuxanoPress.com

Printed by Bookmasters

All Scripture quotations, unless otherwise indicated, are taken from the New American Standard Bible®, Copyright © 1960, 1962, 1963, 1968, 1971, 1972, 1975, 1977, 1995 by The Lockman Foundation. Used by permissions. www.Lockman.org

Scripture quotations marked KJV are taken from the King James Version of the Bible.

What others are saying...

Jim Richards is a leader with a vision and a heart for God. He is also a gifted writer and communicator. In his new book, "Encouraging Words for Difficult Days," Dr. Richards moves with a scholar's precision through the hostile challenges faced by the earliest Christians, then effortlessly applies the biblical situation to unusually similar challenges in our culture today. But beyond merely describing problems, Dr Richards uses the biblical text to prescribe solutions for life today.

This book has arrived just in time. We need it!

J. Kie Bowman, Senior Pastor
Hyde Park Baptist Church
Austin, Texas

In this writing, Jim Richards provides a timely word for Christians today. This study into 1-2 Peter and Jude, addresses key warnings to believers, while encouraging them in their faith journey. Whether reading for your own fulfillment, or delving into a group study, this book will strengthen your faith journey.

Nathan Lino, Senior Pastor
Northeast Houston Baptist Church
President – Southern Baptists of Texas Convention (2016)
Houston, Texas

With the heart of a pastor and the mind of a scholar, Dr. Jim Richards has given the church a tremendous resource, Encouraging Words for Difficult Days: A Study of 1, 2 Peter & Jude. I am grateful to my friend, Dr. Richards, for producing this helpful Bible study, and as you access it, you will be grateful as well.

Dr. Jason K. Allen
President, Midwestern Baptist Theological Seminary

1 & 2 Peter, and Jude, are as important as ever as encouragement and warning to the church. In this short book, Dr. Richards unpacks the letters of Peter and Jude in an easy to read, understandable, and challenging way, with examples from his own life. I highly recommend it!

Matt Carter,
Senior Pastor, The Austin Stone Community Church,
Austin, TX

There are many facets to Dr. Jim Richards' book that I appreciate. He does an excellent job of addressing the biblical text, yes even the tough ones that some might overlook! He gives very helpful explanation and application of the text and offers the reader pertinent and insightful illustrations as well. Jim is one of the most godly men I know and I highly recommend this fine life application commentary on 1 and 2 Peter and Jude. You will be blessed and your walk with God strengthened.

Danny Forshee
Pastor Great Hills Baptist Church,
Austin, TX

Contents

Dedication

My dear friend of over thirty years, Joe Senn, died unexpectedly. He was a loving pastor of a rural church. Joe eternally impacted my life. This book is to all the Lord's servants who serve in small churches and out-of-the-way places. God gives no small assignments. Your faithfulness will be rewarded when we see Jesus.

Foreword

We live today in a world that is hostile to Christian faith and practice. Religious ideas float like plankton on the waves of our culture. The word plankton means wandering or drifting. Such is an apt description of our world today as we are cut loose from all principles and practices that bring sense and wholeness to life. We are slowly sliding into cultural suicide and death. Unbridled restraint and distortion of reality are in open display. Violence, even extreme brutality, characterizes our world; and martyrdom is now common among believers worldwide. Immorality abounds, lying is disregarded and integrity has all but disappeared.

Christianity was born in just such a world. Early believers flourished, and the message of the cross and the resurrection reshaped the world. The books of 1 and 2 Peter and Jude stand as solid witness and strategic importance to believers in our world today.

I have known Jim Richards for over thirty-five years. I have watched him as a pastor and as an associational and a state convention leader. I cherish him as a friend! He has never wavered in his commitment to God and to God's inerrant Word. He stands tall in his leadership in Texas and beyond. His life is a testimony to the reality of genuine discipleship. His covenant marriage to his sweetheart, June, is a prototypi-cal example of what a godly marriage should be. In short, he is real, believable, and consistent. He has opened up this remarkable portion of God's Word in a way that will enlighten, encourage, and challenge those who study it.

God gave us these three books through the Holy Spirit in hard-hitting, no-nonsense fashion. They concisely deal with heretics and heresy, Satan's attacks, and the distortion of God's Word. We find a clear picture of redemption and what is required of believers. We catch a glimpse of the final victory that comes when the Lord returns. We grasp an understanding of suffering as common to us all but also the victory that is ours when we are experiencing it. We are confronted with doctrines like sanctification, the sovereignty of God, humankind's accountability, foreknowledge, and election. We are encouraged to find that transformation of life always occurs when one is genuinely saved. We are deeply impressed to find that love is the supreme gift of God to all believers, and that love impacts the spirit of all believers.

These three books are often neglected but are full of priceless truth and apply to all of our lives. Oh, yes, we are reminded that true believers should always live in deep humility in every relationship in life. You will be blessed as Jim Richards unpacks these truths in a way that is positive, practical, and adequate to hear and understand God's message to us all.

Jimmy Draper
President Emeritus, LifeWay Christian Resources

Acknowledgments

Someone has said writing a book is like giving birth. Of course there is no way for me know the truthfulness of that statement. I did struggle with the material. The depths of God's mind are revealed in 1 Peter. Second Peter and Jude are stark warnings about the dangers of false teaching. Turbulent times require us to fix out attention on God's unwavering truth. If anything benefits you as you read this book, I give all glory to God.

Kenneth Priest continues to be the primary instigator of work. He pushed me along when I lagged behind. I am eternally grateful to him as a colleague and friend. Judi Hayes reviewed the manuscript, providing formation in structure of the writing. A number of others allowed me use them as soundboards through the process. I am grateful for the input of unnamed influences throughout my life.

My wife, June, is my ultimate cheerleader. She encouraged me to the finish line on this book. Without her I would accomplish little. With her help I have been able to stay the course in ministry.

Experiences pastoring small- and medium-size churches proved to be invaluable. Unnamed personalities contributed to my life education. I was able to draw out of these life experiences difficulties and joy that shaped my practical theology.

First and foremost I want to give glory to God for allowing me to complete this book. His grace is ever sufficient. I pray these simple words will help illumine God's Word. May the outcome be that you are more like Jesus.

Introduction to 1 Peter

The fisherman from Galilee became the powerful preacher of the gospel at Pentecost. The one who denied Jesus three times spoke to tens of thousands about the risen Lord. Peter experienced a transformation after the Holy Spirit came upon him. Peter became a different man. Peter was used of God to write a portion of God's Word.

Peter deals with profound doctrines such as election, foreknowledge, sanctification, and the Trinity. These doctrines are intertwined with the words of hope for the suffering saints. Peter was a man who had the reputation of being impetuous. In his writings we see how he became patient.

Scholars debate whether Peter wrote this letter. He said he was in Babylon (1 Pet. 5:13). The Babylon of the Old Testament by the time of the first century was basically a deserted ruin. Some speculate that Peter was talking about Rome. While Peter's location at the time of the writing is not irrelevant, it certainly does not change the message.

Some scholars say Peter wrote to Jews scattered throughout the area of modern-day Turkey. Others say Peter was addressing Gentiles who had come to Christ. Regardless, Peter's words that circulated beyond that region ultimately were passed down to us today. Those words are inspired and preserved by the Holy Spirit.

The first century was a time of persecution for the followers of Jesus. Peter wanted to encourage Christians to remain faithful through trials they were facing. Suffering is mentioned sixteen times in the letter. Peter offers encouraging words for difficult days. Life is challenging. You may be experiencing one of those difficult periods in your life. This letter is just for you.

Chapter 1
In the Mind of Christ
Focal Text: 1 Peter 1:1–5

A story is told of a preacher who wanted to impress his new congregation so he entitled his sermon, "God and Other Subjects." These first verses cover more than I am capable of understanding or much less explaining. There are mysteries about God that we cannot grasp. We can never learn everything there is to know about God. The beginning point of our spiritual journey with Him is to learn about our salvation.

Since we cannot understand everything about God, we must use faith. Peter begins with what has continually been a controversial doctrine, election. We find three thoughts in the mind of God relative to salvation in this passage of Scripture.

Sovereign Selection—"Foreknowledge"
1 Peter 1:2

Theologians are divided into two main camps about the word "foreknowledge." One group believes God looked down through time and saw who would choose to believe and receive eternal life. The other group believes God chose certain people to receive salvation before time ever began.

These two positions also have a number of variations. Ultimately there is Divine initiation and human responsibility.

The Bible says in Jeremiah 1:5, "Before I formed you in the womb I knew you." On the other hand, the Bible says in Romans 10:13, "Whoever will call on the name of the Lord will be saved." The Bible does not contradict itself. Someone has said that when we enter heaven, the sign on the outside will read, "And the Spirit and the bride say, 'Come.' And let the one who hears say, 'Come.' And let the one who is thirsty come; let the one who wishes take the water of life without cost" (Rev. 22:17). Once inside the inscription on the back of the gate will say, "He chose us in Him before the foundation of the world" (Eph. 1:4). This dynamic tension between Divine will and human accountability is found interwoven from Genesis to Revelation.

No illustration can conclusively reveal the Divine plan. We are not going to settle this theological debate until we see Jesus in heaven. But we do know our salvation is not an afterthought to God. In eternity past He was thinking of us. To experience salvation we must have a relationship with God.

Supernatural Salvation
1 Peter 1:2

God initiates the salvation process. God extends His grace to us. The three Persons of the Godhead are all seen in this verse. There is only one God, but He exists in three Persons—

the Father, the Spirit, and the Son. All three persons of the Trinity are involved in the process of providing eternal life.

Salvation is by grace alone, through faith alone, in Christ alone. Any other type of salvation is based on good works. Human effort cannot produce eternal life. God's supernatural work is to transform lives and redeem people for all eternity.

The Holy Spirit brings awareness of our spiritual lostness. Being lost is basically not being where we should be. We should be in an intimate relationship with God. Because of sin, we cannot enter into God's presence. The Holy Spirit convicts of sin, righteousness, and judgment (John 16:8). The Holy Spirit takes us from death to life by spiritually birthing us into God's family (John 3:6). The Holy Spirit comes to live inside us, making our bodies His temple (1 Cor. 6:19). The Creator God who stepped out on nothing and spoke into nothing causing the worlds to come into existence lives within every believer. This boggles my mind.

Sanctification simply means "to be set apart to God." The sanctification being spoken of in this verse refers to the initial and permanent standing we have before God at the time we receive Jesus as our personal Lord and Savior. *Sanctification* can also mean "the daily decisions by a believer to separate from evil things in order to enjoy more of God's fellowship." Final sanctification (sinlessness) will happen when we get to heaven. One way to put it is to say we have been saved, are being saved, and will be saved. We have been saved from the penalty of sin. We are being saved from the power of sin. One day we will be saved from the presence of sin!

The blood of Jesus is the basis for the believer's right standing before God. In the Old Testament believers practiced animal sacrifices to show their faith in God. Although the blood of animals could never give a person right standing with God, the blood pointed to a final sacrifice that would. Hebrews 9:22 says, "Without shedding of blood there is no forgiveness." Old Testament worship called for a priest to sprinkle the blood of an animal on an object called the mercy seat in the holy of holies. Jesus put His blood on the mercy seat in heaven to provide a covering for our sins. This enables us to have a relationship with the Father.

A holy God cannot allow sin to go unpunished. His justice requires it. To wink at sin would demean the character of God. He demanded a payment for sin. If we pay for our sin, we will be eternally separated from God. Only a perfect, sinless sacrifice could satisfy the holiness of God's demand. Jesus lived a life without sin. His shed blood on the cross paid for our sins. His righteousness was transferred to us as our sin was placed on Him (2 Cor. 5:21). Jesus's blood is essential for forgiveness (Eph. 1:7). His bloody death on the cross was not martyrdom. Jesus was not murdered. He laid down His life to give us life. The blood of Jesus is God's wonderful provision for forgiveness.

Spiritual Submission—Obedience
1 Peter 1:2

Jesus is the potential Savior of all but the personal Savior of those who obey the gospel by repenting and believing. We are all responsible for our decisions. God allows people to choose. God uses the preaching of the gospel to produce eternal life (1 Cor. 1:21). Belief or trust in Jesus's blood payment for sin is the personal response that produces an eternal change. Every person is commanded to repent and believe in the resurrected Lord Jesus. We cannot explain the mind of God, but we can experience His grace. God wants to have a relationship with us. We choose whether to say yes or no. A person cannot say yes until the Holy Spirit brings that person to an understanding of the need for Jesus's blood sacrifice. Our part is simply to submit to the risen Lord.

Being born again is a once-in-a-lifetime experience. People do not have to be born again every time they commit a sin. Once we are born into God's family, we have eternal life. Yet obedience to Jesus is a daily decision for every believer too. Our obedience evidences that we have experienced the new birth. Nothing enables us to face difficult times like knowing the true and living God. Peter starts his letter with the foundational truth of the necessity of a right standing with God. Knowing the God of the universe lives inside of us empowers us to be victorious regardless of what comes our way in life. These are encouraging words for difficult days!

Satisfying Security
1 Peter 1:3–5

Peter personally experienced the security of God's love. On the eve of Jesus's crucifixion, Peter denied Him. Jesus never gave up on Peter. Peter was singled out from the other disciples by Jesus to be told about the good news of the resurrection. Peter knew the keeping power of God's salvation.

God is the One who is to be praised for His marvelous salvation. Salvation is by God's grace. If we are saved by God's grace, we are kept by God's grace. We are unable to save ourselves. We are unable to keep ourselves saved. God's power enables us to know we have eternal life.

I am amazed at God's saving grace. Nothing amazes me more than to experience God's keeping grace. Saving grace begins at the moment of salvation, which is a once-in-a-lifetime moment for us. Keeping grace is virtually a daily experience for all of God's children. Three specific expressions of assurance are seen in these verses.

Praise to God (1:4)

The church I grew up in as a child sang the doxology every Sunday. The song has the phrase, "Praise God from whom all blessings flow." God is worthy of all our praise. The word "Blessed" in verse 3 is translated from the Greek word *eulogetos*, from which we get our English word *eulogy*. We think of a eulogy as nice words said at a funeral about the deceased. Originally the word meant "to offer high praise." The psalms are full of praise phrased as blessing the Lord, (Ps. 103:1). God is worthy of all praise!

Because of Jesus's resurrection, we have a living hope. Our modern definition of *hope* robs the word of the intended truth. I am a lifelong fan of the New Orleans Saints football team. I hope they win the Super Bowl next year. This is probably wishful thinking. When the word *hope* is used in the Bible, it is not wishful thinking. Biblical hope means we can have assurance that something will happen. Eternal life and the resurrection of Jesus are absolutes.

Praise to God is always appropriate because of His great mercy. Believers should continually lift up a note of thanks to our Father. The possessions we receive from God are the second expression of assurance.

Possessions from God (1:4)

Possessions are often passed along to children and grandchildren. A will settles a lot of difficulties involved in the succession of an estate. The most important inheritance we can pass along is a life lived for the Lord Jesus. Our Lord Jesus has given us an inheritance with the Father.

Since God is our Father, whatever is His is ours. Jesus made us heirs of all that belongs to Him (Rom. 8:16–17). We'll never see a "for sale" sign on the mansions in heaven. Our reservations are confirmed (John 14:1–3). What belongs to us cannot be transferred to someone else. Our children or grandchildren cannot inherit our relationship with Jesus. We can lose our spiritual rewards earned in this life (2 John 8), but we cannot lose our salvation.

Lawsuits are filed when an estate disposition is contested. Our salvation inheritance cannot be contested. It is reserved in heaven by God Himself. The third expression of assurance is about the power of God's protection.

Power of God (1:5)

Faith accesses salvation, but the power of God protects it. The King James Version of the Bible uses the phrase, "kept by the power of God." The word "kept" is a military term. God stands guard over our salvation. The State Legislature of Texas authorized the building of a depository to store gold. State and private collections of gold coins and bullion will be kept there. While the facility will be extremely well guarded, nothing on this earth is secure from thieves. The omnipotent God is able to keep us saved. No one can steal our salvation. We cannot forfeit our salvation. We are "kept" by the power of God.

Believers have threefold security, the Person of Christ (Col. 3:3), the seal of the Holy Spirit (Eph. 4:30), and the Father's power. I heard a preacher say once that if the devil could get to your soul once you were saved, he would have to fight the Father, swim through the blood of Jesus, and wrestle the Holy Spirit. The preacher concluded by saying that once the devil did all of that he wouldn't want you because he'd be a saved devil. God is able to produce in the end those whom He has redeemed (Eccl. 3:14).

The Greek Word *apokalupsis* is mentioned three times in chapter 1 (vv. 5, 7, 13). It is translated "last time" in verse 5.

Peter wanted the early believers to be assured that no matter what they saw or what they heard, God is faithful. Believers are bombarded by the world, the flesh, and the devil. The power of God stands guard over our salvation during the earthly journey and then throughout eternity.

For Memory and Meditation
"In Him we have redemption through His blood, the forgiveness of our trespasses, according to the riches of His grace." Ephesians 1:7

Chapter 2
The Mystery of Suffering
Focal Text: 1 Peter 1:6–25

When tragedy strikes, most often people ask, "Why?" When tragedy becomes personal, we ask, "Why me?" Suffering is the reoccurring theme of Peter's letter to the believers. Sixteen times Peter refers to suffering in his correspondence. He was trying to prepare his readers for the trials that would be coming their way. He told them to rejoice in trials and suffering. This sounds like a strange response to difficulties.

Because we live in a sin-cursed world, natural calamities and human atrocities happen all too often. Adam brought sin into the world. Because we live in a fallen world, evil people do evil things. Nature is tainted by Adam's fall. What is called natural disasters is basically a part of living in a world that is broken because of sin. Jesus will end sin's effects when we see Him. Until Jesus returns or we leave this world, trials will be a part of our lives.

Suffering by Permission
1 Peter 1:6

When suffering comes, it is not karma, fate, or an impersonal force of nature. Nothing can come our way without God's permission. He allows trials to test us. We are to rejoice that we have been counted worthy to go through a test.

I have to be honest with you—when I was in school, I had to endure tests I really did not want to take. If I had found a way to avoid the test and still pass the class, I would have taken that course of action. In order to move on spiritually, we must take and pass some tests. First Peter 4:19 says, "Therefore, those also who suffer according to the will of God shall entrust their souls to a faithful Creator in doing what is right." Suffering according to the will of God sounds odd. God allows us to go through the crucible of trials. We are to praise Him that He counts us worthy to take the test.

Showing What You're Made Of (1:7)
God puts us through the fire to refine our faith. Our faith is compared to the refining of gold. A smelter heats the furnace to separate the impurities from the metal. The finished product is valuable—pure gold. Our faith becomes purer by going through trials. The dross of sin is burned away. Suffering demonstrates the genuineness of our faith. The end result will please God at the coming of Jesus.

I saw a preacher once who had an orange on the pulpit. He asked, "If I squeeze this orange, what will come out?" Everyone said orange juice. He injected some black ink into the orange. When he squeezed the orange, dark, sticky ooze came out. What is on the inside will come to the outside. If you squeeze an orange, you will get orange juice. If something else is on the inside, it will come out too. The evidence of Jesus's living in you is more clearly seen when you get squeezed by the trials of this world. For the believer walking with the Lord during a trial, Jesus will come out.

Someone has suggested that if Christians were free from suffering, people would become Christians to escape suffering. A follower of Jesus Christ is not immune to suffering. Often the opposite is the case. Much of the health-and-wealth preacher's message is based on a suffering-free zone for believers. Nothing could be further from the truth. Believers suffer just like anyone else. The difference in our suffering is that it gives us an opportunity to show that Jesus is on the inside. Suffering can be turned into glorifying God.

Seeing the Unseen (1:8–9)

Peter had seen Jesus in the flesh. Virtually none of the recipients of his letter knew Jesus during His time on earth. Instead of "seeing is believing," Peter said that "believing is seeing." When our trust is placed in Jesus, a relationship is established that gives us joy during our earthly journey. We can rejoice in the prospect of the completion of salvation at the coming of Jesus Christ.

The reference to "souls" encompasses the entire person. This is not referring to a disembodied spirit floating around on the clouds. The completion of our faith results in a resurrection that produces a glorified body similar to Jesus's resurrection body. We will be with Him for eternity.

Matchless Witness of God's Word
1 Peter 1:10–25

Nothing can enable us to overcome suffering or trials like abiding in the Word of God. Peter points his readers to the Scriptures as the strength for life. God's Word transforms and energizes so we are able to be victorious in this life.

Old Testament Prophesy (1:10–12)

Old Testament prophets and believers were constantly looking for the promised Messiah. Old Testament writers were overshadowed by the Holy Spirit to write Holy Scripture. Writers were inspired; yet sometimes they did not grasp the import of their own writings. Some did not completely comprehend the full message they were penning. Daniel 12:8 says, "As for me, I heard but could not understand." Daniel was saying that he was relaying the Word of God, but he was not able to grasp what God was conveying. Daniel and others had to seek God for understanding even as they transmitted the Word of God. Without contradiction we can say the "words" were inspired.

The Old Testament saints looked for the Christ anticipating God's grace. The Holy Spirit used the Old Testament to confirm the gospel to those in the first century. The apostles proclaimed the gospel of Jesus Christ enabling Peter's readers to experience what Old Testament Saints had long desired.

The phrase "things into which angels long to look" (v. 12) stirs my curiosity. Angels cannot be saved. When angels rebelled with Satan, they had no provision for their redemption. Furthermore, angels are amazed that the second Person of the Godhead, the Lord Jesus Christ, would leave the glories of heaven to walk the earth as a man. Heavenly beings worship the Triune God. That Jesus would come to earth for the purpose of dying in the place of sinful humanity is incomprehensible to them. We can be thankful that we can sing the song of the redeemed. It is a song the angels cannot sing.

Holiness Is Possible (1:13–23)

Doctrine is of eternal importance. What we believe determines where we will be after this life. What we believe should be reflected in our lives. While biblical apologetics have their place, few people are converted by argument. The best argument we can give in many cases is to live a life of holiness. God calls us to be set apart from the world's culture. We are to progress in our walk with God as evidence that we truly have been born again.

Example of Holiness (1:13–16)

The often-told joke about the word *therefore* is that when we find it in the Bible we should see what it is "there for." Joking aside, when we see the word *therefore* in the Bible, it points us back to prior statements. In the case of verse 13, Peter is referring to all of the preceding statements concerning salvation, Scripture, and the second coming of

Christ. Believers are to pursue holy living as previously stated doctrinal realities.

Grace is the key to walking with God. "Fix your hope completely on the grace . . . of Jesus Christ" (v. 13). This verse confirms that our ability to live a life pleasing to the Father is dependent on His grace. Being crucified with Christ or considering ourselves to be dead to sin is possible when we are fixed on the grace of Jesus.

Jesus is coming again. The apostle John affirms Peter's words by saying, "And everyone who has this hope fixed on Him purifies himself, just as He is pure" (1 John 3:3). Looking for the return of our Lord Jesus cleans us up. The daily expectation of the return of Jesus will prompt us to holy living. We want to be ready to go into His presence when we are convinced that Jesus could come at any moment. Jesus's imminent return is a purifying hope.

God's holiness is the template for our lives. He wants us to be like Him. In verse 16, Peter quotes an Old Testament passage that could be any one of a number from Leviticus (11:44–45; 19:2; 20:7, 26). The concept of God's holiness in the Old Testament was well grounded. To be like God is only possible by the grace of the Lord Jesus.

Expressions of Holiness (1:17–25)
Judgment is coming. Fear is a valid motivator. Some say that once we come to Christ love should be the only motivator. I agree that love should be the primary impetus in our relationship with God. God as our Father is tender and kind.

God is also the impartial Judge of our works. Fear is a valid emotion when it is reverential respect for the One who saved us.

Peter declared the emptiness of the religion of those reading his letter. Peter points to the blood of Jesus as the only way to God. Jesus is the spotless lamb as pictured in the Old Testament offerings. Again, numerous references in Leviticus detail the bloody sacrifice of a perfect lamb as the only acceptable offering to God. Jesus is the only person who ever lived on this earth without committing a sin. Jesus alone satisfies the requirements for our sin covering. He did it for us. He expresses holiness for all.

In verses 21–22, Peter talks about the greatest gifts—faith, hope, and love. Scholars have suggested that the three major New Testament writers each had a dominant theme. Some have suggested that Paul is the apostle of faith, Peter is the apostle of hope, and John is the apostle of love. This is a nice way to remember the emphasis of each writer. Of course, all three presented the truth found in various expressions. Peter underscored that our hope is in the work of Christ.

Jesus's provision was not an afterthought with God. Jesus is not an ambulance on the way to an accident. Jesus is the Lamb slain from the foundation of the world (Rev. 13:8). He is now the resurrected Lord. Because our faith is in Him, our lives should express the holiness by love.

There are questions I have to ask myself daily: Do I have the appropriate gratitude for the price He paid to redeem me? Am I living the life that exhibits my appreciation for the worth of Jesus's provision? Since I am bought by Jesus's blood, do I love God and love others as I should?

When I was pastor of a small country church, I saw a number of expressions of love through holiness. One particular incident has stayed with me through the years. Sam was a man who was known for his roughness. He got into an altercation with George, a retired law enforcement officer, at a local bar. George was almost killed. George vowed he would get even with Sam. This is a strange way to start a love-through-holiness story.

Shortly after this incident, George joined the church where I was the pastor. He said he was saved but had wandered away. Within a few months Sam was seriously injured at work. He was not expected to live. A layman in the church asked me to visit Sam in intensive care. Although Sam could not talk, he responded by squeezing my hand. I shared the gospel with Sam. He indicated through squeezing my hand that he accepted Christ. I thought Sam would never make it out of the hospital alive.

Sam not only lived, but as soon as he was able, he visited every church that had prayed for him. Sam told me he wanted me to baptize him. I dreaded the day Sam came to church because George sat on the third row every Sunday.

When Sam came to church, he sat in the back. At the invitation Sam came forward. I presented him to the church without making eye contact with George. I was not sure what would happen. George was at the end of the reception line for Sam. Would he hit him? Would he pull a gun or knife? What was going to happen?

Finally, George stood face-to-face with Sam. They stared at each other for what seemed like forever. George extended his hand to Sam. Sam embraced George. Only Jesus could produce that type of love. Salvation produces love for the brethren. The holiness of Jesus enables the love for one another.

Verse 23 tells us that salvation is possible by the work of the Word of God and the Holy Spirit.

In verses 24–25, Peter quoted the Old Testament prophet, Isaiah. Isaiah 40:7–8 says, "The grass withers, the flower fades, when the breath of the LORD blows upon it; surely the people are grass. The grass withers, the flower fades, but the word of our God stands forever." This Old Testament prophecy was a promise of deliverance and victory for Israel. When persecutors seem invincible, God is able to help us withstand whatever may come our way. Because we have been partakers of the divine nature by receiving Christ, we are assured of victory in Jesus. Persecutors do not have the final say. There is a time coming when they will answer to the Word of God.

For Memory and Meditation
"Like the Holy One who called you, be holy yourselves also in all *your* behavior." 1 Peter 1:15

Chapter 3
The Believer's Lifestyle
Focal Text: 1 Peter 2:1–12

When people become believers, they often experience a dramatic lifestyle shift. Outward actions and inward attitudes are affected. This does not mean believers will no longer struggle with sin. They will. Like Paul they will often say: "I am of flesh, sold into bondage to sin. For what I am doing, I do not understand; for I am not practicing what I *would* like to *do*, but I am doing the very thing I hate" (Rom. 7:14–15).

But when a person becomes a believer, like Paul, their *desire* to behave differently changes. A difference takes place when a person first understands and believes that Christ came to save. He came to save all. Then a believer will experience a noticeable change. If a person becomes a believer in Jesus at age nine, of course, fewer overt sins may be obvious than for a person who is a thirty-nine-year-old drug dealer and first feels the personal power of the gospel message. However, the common thread in everyone's conversion is a desire to obey Jesus. Jesus said, "If you love Me, you will keep My commandments" (John 14:15).

Salvation is not so much the change in actions as it is the change in attitude. New believers shift allegiance. They seek to move self from the throne and to obey Christ because of

His great love for them. They desire to love and obey Him in return.

LifeStyle Changes
1 Peter 2:1–5

Seismic Change (2:1)

Most people can conform to some type of legalistic moral code for a brief period. Paul often wrote about the shift from law to grace. In Romans 7:6, Paul wrote, "But now we have been released from the Law, having died to that by which we were bound, so that we serve in newness of the Spirit and not in oldness of the letter." But both Peter and Paul point out specific sins—forbidden under the law but still evident in believers' lives—which, as we grow in Christ, we should not do.

The discipline to maintain strict obedience to the law is difficult. Early in chapter 2, Peter mentions some of the sins believers should put aside. After all, new believers may not yet know that some of their specific behaviors are displeasing to God. But when we become aware of them, we should seek to change.

Malice—the first sin Peter mentions—is an unforgiving spirit. Removing malice is a challenge even for believers. Guile is the intent to manipulate in order to get even with those who have wronged us. Someone has said, "I don't get even; I get ahead." The only way to get ahead for the gospel is to have the heart change that produces a kind, gentle spirit. A bitter spirit produces more pain. God is the One who will avenge. Justice will come in this life or the next.

Similarly, Peter says new believers should be putting aside… all deceit and hypocrisy and envy and all slander."

Signs of Conversion (2:2–5)

A crying baby may indicate many needs. Some babies cry because they want to be held. We start out in life wanting attention. Some babies cry because they need a diaper change. Some babies cry because they are in pain. Our hearts are broken when little can be done to alleviate the suffering of a small child or a baby. Oftentimes babies cry when they are hungry. We come into this world with a need for nourishment. Life is sustained by proper nutrients. Peter uses the analogy of the physical baby's need for food to the spiritual baby's desiring the milk of the Word of God. A spiritual baby's growth depends on receiving the milk of God's Word. Tragically some babies do not develop properly. Sadly, many spiritual babies never develop either. At the moment of salvation, a person will have an immediate hunger for spiritual food. The spiritual baby needs to be cared for properly, just as an infant does. Working with new converts calls for sacrificial attention to their needs. We call it discipleship.

Mothers are usually so attentive to their young children that they can distinguish one cry from another and know right away just what their babies need. As more mature believers work with or mentor new believers, we should get to know them so we can develop trust and help them in their specific areas of need. That's one reason new believers need to be part of a church—the family of God, the family of faith. As members of the faith community, new believers find many family members who will guide them and help them grow, healing their hurts and feeding their hunger to grow in Christlikeness.

When we taste "the kindness of the Lord," we experience His grace. No one can produce the sweetness of forgiveness like our Lord Jesus. Because of God's mercy, we can enjoy full fellowship with our heavenly Father.

Peter uses other analogies to describe the new believer. Peter said believers are "living stones" and "a holy priesthood." In replacing the temple and the Aaronic priesthood as the center of worship, those who have come to Christ now provide continual worship of the Lord Jesus. Corporate, congregational worship is expected of every believer. Unlike the Old Testament worship system, New Testament believers can worship without a specific structure. It is not the place of worship but the people of worship that makes a congregation a church.

Only a select few could be priests in the Old Testament. The priest went into the temple to go to God for the people. Worshippers were dependent on a priest to make sacrifices and offerings for them. Without a priest, the people could not enter into corporate worship. Because of Jesus each individual believer now is considered a priest unto God. We have immediate access to the Father because of what Jesus did for us on the cross. Also, He is our high priest. Hebrews 4:14 says, "Seeing then that we have a great high priest that is passed to the heavens, Jesus the Son of God, let us hold fast our profession" (KJV). We do not go through a priest or religious system to get to God. Jesus makes intercession for us. Jesus is in heaven to plead our case. First Timothy 2:5 declares, "For there is one God, and one mediator between God and men, the man Christ Jesus" (KJV). We become priests in our own right because of Jesus. As our high priest, Jesus carries our petitions and praise to the Father for us.

The Savior Is the Cornerstone
1 Peter 2:6–8

Jesus became the chief cornerstone of a spiritual temple God is building. All who come to Christ in faith are a part of the spiritual superstructure. Peter quotes Isaiah 28:16, "Therefore thus says the Lord God, 'Behold, I am laying in Zion a stone, a tested stone, a costly cornerstone for the foundation, firmly placed. He who believes in it will not be disturbed.'" Psalm 118:22 is a prophetic witness, "The stone which the builders rejected has become the chief corner stone." Paul used the same reference in his letter to the Romans (Rom. 9:33). Jesus quoted the same psalm in Matthew 21:42.

The cornerstone in the foundation had to be perfectly cut. The importance of the cornerstone was to be the reference for all other stones in a structure. All of the other stones would be set in alignment with the cornerstone. The integrity of a structure depended on the proper placing of the cornerstone. A cornerstone could be rejected for various reasons. Any type of flaw would cause a cornerstone to be discarded. Jesus was the perfect cornerstone. The religious leaders of the Old Testament worship did not think Jesus fit. They rejected Him because He did not fit the Old Testament structure of worship. Jesus became the chief cornerstone of a new spiritual building, the glorious church. Everyone who comes to Christ is placed properly because He is the Chief Cornerstone setting the pattern for all who follow Him.

Peter quotes Isaiah 8:14, "A stone to strike and a rock to stumble over." This is a warning to those who reject Jesus. Unbelievers will find themselves rejected. Christ is the living stone who is the cornerstone. He alone can make a stone a living stone. People will either see Jesus as a cornerstone of faith or a stumbling block to their own desires. He can bring to life those who are dead in sin. He is the exceptional Christ.

Special Creation
1 Peter 2:9–12

Peter uses four descriptive terms to show a new position for the person in Christ: "a chosen race, a royal priesthood, a holy nation, a people for God's own possession." Encompassed in these terms is the creation of a new kind of people.

God made Abraham the first Jew. When we get in Christ, we are a part of a new spiritual race. Both Jews and Gentiles comprise this new race. The Greek word *ethnos* is translated "nation" in the NASB. It is the word from which we get the

English word *ethnic*. Being "a holy nation" is not a geopolitical distinction. A believer's spiritual ethnicity is Christian. We are followers of Jesus. One day we will all be in heaven at the throne of God. Revelation 7:9 predicts the day is coming, "After these things I looked, and behold, a great multitude which no one could count, from every nation and *all* tribes and peoples and tongues, which no one could number, standing before the throne and before the Lamb."

Having a spiritual ethnicity does not remove us from earthly obligations. The apostle Paul used his Roman citizenship to further the gospel. Some people lose the balance of living in this world while keeping their affections on Christ. Years ago I heard it put this way, "He is so heavenly minded that he is no earthly good." We can unrealistically approach life cloistered in a monastery. We are citizens of heaven, but we have an obligation in this life. We are to live in the world system but not be like the world system. After coming to Christ, we are to proclaim His grace to others. We are also to participate in the affairs of this life too.

We looked at the priesthood previously. To hear proclaimed that we are "God's own possession" should give us boldness to live for Jesus. We are owned by the Creator of the universe. Because we have been transformed from death to life, we have a story to tell.

Having already established that believers are now different from the world system, Peter's challenge is to give evidence by abstaining from participating in sinful practices. Involvement in questionable activities drains a person's spiritual strength.

Living out a testimony before unbelievers is essential for a verbal witness. We are to share the gospel verbally. If we have a spoiled lifestyle, people will have difficulty hearing what we have to say. Charles Spurgeon, the great eighteenth-century preacher, had a training school for those entering the ministry. On occasion Spurgeon spoke about an eloquent preacher who did not live what he preached. He recorded this story in *Lectures to My Students*. Spurgeon commented, "He preached so well that when he was in the pulpit people said he should never leave. He lived so poorly that when he was out of it, that he should never get into it." Spurgeon said a preacher who did not live what he preached was "like a stained glass window. It does not let the light shine clearly."

Unbelievers will slander the people of God. It is incumbent on believers to live a consistent Christlike life. The hope is that some of the unbelievers will be saved, which will prepare them for the coming of Christ.

For Memory and Meditation
"But you are a chosen race, a royal priesthood, a holy nation, a people for *God's* own possession, so that you may proclaim the excellencies of Him who has called you out of darkness into His marvelous light." 2 Peter 2:9

Chapter 4
Social Change through the Gospel
Focal Text: 1 Peter 2:13–25

Some of the most impactful instructions in Peter's letter are found in this section of his first letter. Most areas of human interaction are covered in these directives. These words challenge our attitudes. They call us to action.

The American context of government is very different from that of the first-century Roman Empire. Despotic emperors ruled the Roman world with little regard to morality. No organization of government provided any kind check on their power. Jews had been ordered out of Rome near the time of Peter's letter. The government tolerated most religions. Religions found unacceptable were those calling for exclusivity in worship and loyalty. Jews, and later Christians, would fall under Roman persecution because of their claim to worship only one God, the true God of the Scriptures. To proclaim Caesar as Lord was unacceptable to both Jews and Christians.

This allegiance to the one true God and not to any governmental leader is seen throughout the Old Testament. Recall in the book of Daniel, for example, the refusal of Shadrach, Meshach, and Abed-nego to bow down to the golden statue of Nebuchadnezzar, the Babylonian king.

These three Jews, like Daniel, were in Babylon, having been taken there in captivity. Holding on to their faith, they refused to give any appearance of worshipping the image of this king. For their faithfulness they were thrown into a den of lions. And like these three young men, New Testament Jews, and later Christians, who refused to worship the current Roman emperor faced serious persecution and even death.

Slavery was also practiced in the Roman Empire. Like the governmental system, slavery in the Roman Empire differed from the American experience. Nevertheless, it was still oppressive. Little regard was held for human life. Human dignity was virtually absent. Class structure was enforced rigidly. Any social action to change the status quo would have been interpreted as an insurrection against the government. This would have spelled doom for the fledgling early church. Rather than trying to change the system, the believers in Jesus pursued a course to win one person at a time. By overcoming the system with the influence of the gospel, the social ills would be rectified. Paul's friendship with one slave, Onesimus, is the subject of the small letter of Philemon, and Onesimus is mentioned in other places in the New Testament. In Galatians 3:28–29, Paul wrote, "There is neither Jew nor Greek, there is neither slave nor free man, there is neither male nor female; for you are all one in Christ Jesus. And if you belong to Christ, then you are Abraham's descendants, heirs according to promise." Christ did not come to save only the Jews, only the wealthy, or only the men of society. Both Paul and Peter stressed that all believers are one in Christ.

A third societal topic Peter addressed was the family. Husband and wife relationships in most cases in the Roman world were more like a master to a servant. Lower social-status women had almost no rights. Jewish culture had devolved to a point that a man could divorce his wife for any one of a number of frivolous reasons. Men ruled the home with absolute authority. New Testament biblical Christianity stood these positions on their head.

Some scholars say this section reflects a common theme in the ancient world for societal order. The apostle Paul gave similar approaches to the social order in several of his letters. These behavioral guidelines are labeled the "household codes" because topics related to husband and wife are included.

Under the inspiration of the Holy Spirit, Peter wrote an infallible guide to living out our faith in a hostile environment. The sufficiency of Scriptures gives us confidence that the principles found in dealing with issues twenty centuries ago continue to be applicable today.

Submission to Governmental Authority
1 Peter 2:13–17

The king referred to in the passage has to be Caesar. Caesar had absolute authority. Although Caesar persecuted Christians, Caesar's position of authority was to be respected. When Americans have a president or a Supreme Court ruling that conflicts with biblical truth, we—especially as believers who want to give a positive witness by our behavior in all circumstances—are to be respectful even if we disagree. Because Americans have a system of redress (voting), it is the obligation and the privilege of every believer to pursue righteousness as much as possible when selecting a leader. First-century believers did not have an opportunity to influence leadership through the ballot box. They were commanded to respect the ruler. Most people think a country's rulers are supposed to punish evil and promote what is right. But God's ideal is often obscured by human sinfulness.

God's will for every believer is to do what is right by God's standards. When ignorant accusations come, a believer's correct conduct is the answer. Christians were continually under scrutiny in the Roman era, and many believers today experience the same kind of close examination of everything they do. Worship of Caesar was the norm. For a believer to reject Caesar worship meant the believer had to go the extra mile to prove he had no evil intent toward the government. Unless violating biblical truth (Acts 5:29), the believer was to submit to governmental authority. When submitting to authority, the believer offered up praise to God. Believers are free, but their freedom is to obey God first, then to obey those God has ordained.

Jesus set the standard in how believers should relate to others. In His Sermon on the Mount, Jesus talked about a variety of relationships, including these situations: "Do not resist an evil person; but whoever slaps you on your right cheek, turn the other to him also. If anyone wants to sue you and take your shirt, let him have your coat also. Whoever forces you to go one mile, go with him two. Give to him who asks of you, and do not turn away from him who wants to borrow from you" (Matt. 5:39–42).

Peter summarizes the way believers should act in four commands found in verse 17: "Honor all people, love the brotherhood, fear God, honor the king." All persons deserve respect and dignity. Everyone is created in God's image— even your enemies, even those who persecute you, even the king. Remember Jesus said, "Blessed are those who have been persecuted for the sake of righteousness, for theirs is the kingdom of heaven. Blessed are you when *people* insult you and persecute you, and falsely say all kinds of evil against you because of Me. Rejoice and be glad, for your reward in heaven is great; for in the same way they persecuted the prophets who were before you" (Matt. 5:10–12).

Believers share a special bond. We are to express a unique affinity toward others in the family of God. The word "brotherhood" appears in the New Testament only twice, both times in 1 Peter. Caesar is to be honored, but only God is to be feared. Ultimate loyalty belongs to God, not the emperor, masters, or husbands.

Submission to Workplace Authority
1 Peter 2:18–25

Sometimes pastors and teachers apply this passage to our modern-day workplace setting. Using the principles for employee-employer relationship is helpful. Being in a difficult job calls upon a believer to live out his faith to the glory of God. And in good working conditions, Christian employees should use their time and the company's resources honestly and wisely, representing Christ in the workplace rather than take advantage of a lenient boss.

Slavery was practiced throughout the Greco-Roman world. The historical setting of the text was very different from the American experience of slavery. American slavery was built on an economic system that demanded free labor. In the first century people became slaves after losing a war, being kidnapped from a foreign country, or being born as a slave. People actually sold themselves into slavery due to economic hardship. Many slaves lived miserable lives. They labored in the fields, on ships, and in mines. The conditions for many slaves were intolerably inhuman. Slaves had no legal standing. Masters could beat their slaves. Household slaves fared better. Some were better educated than their masters. A process existed for slaves to buy their freedom, but for most slaves freedom from slavery was an unrealistic dream. The slave who became a believer was to live out his life as a testimony for the Lord Jesus, even while continuing in slavery.

Peter did not address the evil of slavery. Why? This is a question many of us would ask. The New Testament writers equip believers with the tools to live in a sinful world system. Railing against slavery in the first century would have been no help to the Christian caught in its snare. Peter, like other New Testament writers, concerned himself with the relationship between individuals and God. These writers of Gospels and letters focused on how the believer is to show a godly response to mistreatment. Of course, if enough individuals come to Christ, the culture can be transformed.

Peter was not saying that Christian slaves were to participate in evil or follow a master in a sinful act. He was pointing out that slaves could not refuse a master's commands on the basis that the master was evil. Unless conscience was violated, the Christian slave was to do what he or she was told. Slaves should represent Christ well, and they had no reason to put themselves in a position to be punished for disobedience when the master's command did not violate biblical truth.

If punishment came because of obedience to God or unjustly at the hands of the master, the slave would find favor with God. The example of Jesus's sufferings provided a template for slaves to endure harshness from a master.

Principles for living in our modern society apply. Employee-employer relations can be measured by the teachings in this section about slavery. Some people suffer through difficult workplace pressures. We are told to be a witness wherever we find ourselves, even in daily adverse workplace situations.

To imitate Christ during His unjust indescribable suffering is the pinnacle of the Christian calling. Our "calling" is the Greek word *eklethete*, which refers to God's calling upon the believer for salvation. Suffering is a part of the salvation journey for believers. Peter quotes Isaiah 53:9 to illustrate

Jesus's sinlessness in the face of suffering: "His grave was assigned with wicked men, yet He was with a rich man in His death, because He had done no violence, nor was there any deceit in His mouth." By the time Peter wrote this letter, Isaiah 53 had become an acceptable text to point people to the Suffering Messiah, Jesus. Jesus's example shows believers—then as well as today—that they should follow His example by refraining from sin when mistreated as His disciples.

Jesus' suffering was unique. Jesus died a bloody, sacrificial, substitutionary death on the cross. No one else could have done it. He provided salvation for those who would believe. Peter returns to Isaiah for a reference (2:24), describing Jesus's sufferings: "But He was pierced through for our transgressions, He was crushed for our iniquities; the chastening for our well-being fell upon Him, and by His scourging we are healed" (Isa. 53:5). The implication of Jesus's death was not only to provide forgiveness of sin but also to enable believers to live a righteous life. This does not mean believers will be sinless. It does mean that because of Jesus believers can live a different kind of life. Power to live a godly life and endure suffering for Jesus's sake is available because of the cross. Jesus suffered for us. Now we are privileged to suffer for Him. Jesus is our Shepherd. The word *shepherd* comes from the Greek word *episkopos*. The Greek word is translated "overseer" or "bishop" in English translations. Jesus is the overseer or authority over our souls.

For Memory and Meditation

"For what credit is there if, when you sin and are harshly treated, you endure it with patience? But if when you do what is right and suffer *for it* you patiently endure it, this *finds* favor with God." 1 Peter 2:20

Chapter 5
Godly Living
Focal Test: 1 Peter 3:1–12

As Peter continues to instruct believers, he does not limit his instructions to those living—and perhaps being persecuted—in a government that has turned its back on God or to slaves. Twenty-first-century believers apply the instruction in chapter 2 to people in all government settings and to employee-employer relationships. In chapter 3 Peter turns his attention to the home and the church. In these situations—just as in the ones described in the previous chapter—*submission* is the chosen word.

You know, just the word *submission* can make a lot of folks bristle today. It's not a very popular word. People seem to think submission is something one person makes another do. It's not. People have to choose to be submissive, to yield to another. In dying on the cross, Jesus submitted to God's will and way to save people from their sins so they can live in relationship with Him on earth and throughout eternity. Believers today submit to one another as they dwell in the grace of God's forgiveness. In difficult, oppressive situations, some people may choose to submit to avoid punishment, but even then they can endure and survive in Jesus's love.

In love, Jesus submitted to God. In love, people in families submit to one another. In Christian love, people in church submit to one another. Submission demonstrates Christlike behavior. Maybe some of us should give submission another chance.

Submission to Authority in the Home
1 Peter 3:1–7

Human rights are based in the Word of God. Civil rights are an outgrowth of human rights in most cases. Feminism allowing women suffrage, equal pay for equal work, and other American ideals are right and should be affirmed by Christians. Feminism declaring a woman can do whatever she wishes with her own body does not include newly created human beings in her womb. The taking of human life in the womb is morally and biblically unacceptable. Feminism that diminishes the man's role in the home as the spiritual leader is contrary to Scripture. Controversy surrounds the subject of husband and wife relations in churches. Peter entered the controversy from a different perspective.

During the time of the writing of this letter, women were oppressed. Often women were treated more like property. Peter was reinforcing the spiritual equality of women with men. He saw women holding a unique place in the husband-and-wife relationship. He said women have a calling to fulfill.

The "household code" part of Peter's letter focuses on the one who is under authority. The text speaks about submission "in the same way" (3:1) as a slave to a master or a citizen to the government. Nowhere does the New Testament teach that women are inferior to men. Women are seen as coheirs of eternal life with their husbands. Throughout the New Testament women were elevated from a low cultural position to one of equality with men. The submission of wives is a theological truth illustrating the relationship of Christ and the church. The apostle Paul drew this clear distinction in Ephesians 5:22–33. Transcending the culture of the first century, the New Testament teaching shows the submission of wives to husbands as a mirror to the church's submission to Jesus.

Have you known Christians who thought they were better than those who were not? Have you known believers who looked down on people they considered beneath them? Have you known people who called themselves Christians who condemned evildoers? They were called Pharisees in Jesus's day. They didn't know much about love, grace, mercy, submission, or God's concern for "the least of these." How can such an attitude persuade any unbeliever to be a Christian? Peter's call to be submissive counteracts this holier-than-thou attitude.

Speaking directly to women whose husbands were unbelievers, Peter tells the wives that they could very well hold the key to their husband's salvation. Peter was calling for more than outward acts of obedience but a holy lifestyle before God with a sweet spirit. A woman's godly behavior is the primary influence on unbelieving husbands.

Outward sex appeal will not convince the unbelieving husband to trust Christ. Every couple should keep the "honey in the honeymoon." Staying attentive to the needs of our spouse is part of honoring Christ too. However, the outward appearance fades, but the inward beauty lasts a lifetime.

"Hope in God" meant the women were to submit not because their husbands were superior to them intellectually or spiritually but because they were confident that God would reward them. Peter continued to underscore the hope that produces contentment in this life. Suffering cannot extinguish hope. Persecution cannot kill hope. A better day is coming where faithfulness to the Lord will be rewarded.

Peter appealed to the wives of the patriarchs as examples of godly submission. Sarah was the one he singled out as a template. Sarah's trust in God empowered her to submit to her husband. Sarah followed Abraham's leadership. Sarah put her faith in God when she agreed to Abraham's directives, even when it placed her in unfavorable conditions (see Gen. 12 and 20).

By living a faithful Christian life, a woman has a stronger possibility of winning her unsaved husband to Christ. As in all submission, the submission of a wife to her husband has limits. Absolute submission is not implied in Scripture. If a husband requires a wife to violate biblical truth or follow another faith system, then the wife should disobey. First-century women were expected to take the religion of their husbands. Peter was introducing a socially radical idea. Jesus always comes first.

Only one verse in this section speaks to husbands about their responsibilities in the home relationship. Husbands are to be the spiritual leaders. Husbands are to know the way of God. Husbands are to lead in finding God's will for the family. The reference about women being "someone weaker" is primarily addressing the general physical stature of women. Being an equal recipient of eternal life, the wife is to receive honor. The husband who lives according to God's expectation will show respect to his wife. God holds husbands accountable for the treatment of their wives. A position of authority is to be used for spiritual blessing, not to give license for abuse and mistreatment of those under their watch. Husbands who disregard God's plan for the husband-wife relationship can experience spiritual failure.

Nowhere are husbands directed to submit to their wives. The New Testament passages that address husband-and-wife relationships speak to husbands about their accountability in the treatment of their wives. Little is said about the responsibility of those who hold governmental or ownership authority. In the husband-and-wife relationship there is a definitive shift to the leaders' obligations.

If some people might think this is one-sided, consider Paul's words in Ephesians 5: "Wives, *be subject* to your own husbands, as to the Lord. . . . Husbands, love your wives, just as Christ also loved the church and gave Himself up for her" (vv. 22, 25). The instructions to both husbands and wives are equally demanding.

God sets a high standard for relationships. Whether in government, the workplace, or the home, God will not bless those in authority who mistreat those for whom they are responsible. Social justice is achieved by living out the life of Christ.

Submission to One Another as the Church
1 Peter 3:8–12

In the Greco-Roman worldview of the first century, submission was looked upon with disdain. Meekness was seen as weakness. Twenty-first-century American culture continues to admire individuals who are audacious. Arrogant public figures dominate the news. Graciousness is viewed with suspicion. People who don't try to climb to the top of the heap—no matter who gets trampled in the process—are sometimes seen as losers. Not much has changed in the past two thousand years.

Peter wraps up his comments on submission with an appeal to believers. Believers who choose to submit to one another in the church show the love of Christ. The distinctiveness of living for Jesus speaks to a broken world. Believers responding to the world by submission project a testimony far louder than words. Believers offer a contrast the world cannot understand.

Inside the Assembly (3:8)
In the original language of the Bible, we find five adjectives in this verse without a verb. In the NASB these adjectives are "harmonious, sympathetic, brotherly, kindhearted, and

humble in spirit." And Peter has added an implied imperative to all of these words. Faith living produces action. Harmony calls for unity in the church.

Division in the church is not a new phenomenon, but it is an unnecessary one. Jesus wanted to set believers apart by their love for one another. He said, "A new commandment I give to you, that you love one another, even as I have loved you, that you also love one another. By this all men will know that you are My disciples, if you have love for one another" (John 13:34–35). He prayed that His followers would be united, both the Twelve and His followers in all generations: "I do not ask on behalf of these alone, but for those also who believe in Me through their word; that they may all be one; even as You, Father, *are* in Me and I in You, that they also may be in Us, so that the world may believe that You sent Me" (John 17:30–21). Paul echoed Jesus's desire for unity: "Be devoted to one another in brotherly love; give preference to one another in honor" (Rom. 12:10).

Sympathy toward other believers means to share in the ups and downs of life. Brotherly kindness is the centerpiece of this appeal for submission in the church. Every believer is in the family of God. We have the brother-sister relationship making us knit together through a blood relationship, the blood of Christ. The word "kindhearted" is translated from a Greek word that means to express compassion toward those who are experiencing pain. To be "humble" is to consider others more important that yourself. This verse is summed up in the words of Jesus when He said, "Love your neighbor as yourself" (Matt. 22:39). And seen again in Paul's letter to the

Romans: "Be kind to one another, tender-hearted, forgiving each other, just as God in Christ also has forgiven you" (Eph. 4:32).

Outside the Assembly (3:9–12)

Jesus taught His followers to do good to those who mistreated them. An "eye for an eye" was replaced with "turn the other cheek" (see Matt. 5:38–39). Peter was saying that when we react to those who mistreat us with a blessing, we are giving more evidence that we have experienced eternal life. Trying to get payback on someone who has mistreated us is the antithesis of a Christlike spirit. A heart that beats in rhythm with Jesus's heart will not seek retaliation.

Peter paraphrases the Old Testament in verses 10–12. Peter uses a quote from Psalm 34:15–16 to point out that God hears the prayers of believers. The persecutor is the one the Lord will not hear. Psalm 34 reflects a time of distress in the life of David. It tells how God is able to sustain His children through suffering. He can deliver us from a trial. He can enable us to go through the trial. The believer is not only to refrain from speaking evil but also to do good, especially by seeking peace.

Some disparage the "sinner's prayer" found in Luke 18:13. Jesus was using a parable about two men praying. One was extolling his own virtues. He was proud of his religious practices. The other man would not even lift his head but simply cried out, "God, be merciful to me a sinner." Jesus said the latter was justified while the former was not. The only prayer a sinner can pray that will surely be heard by God is the "sinner's prayer." It is not the prayer that saves us but Jesus. However, even a nonverbal prayer needs to exhibit the broken spirit of the sinful man at the temple.

Peter was giving encouragement to those coming under persecution. He assured them a sovereign God was attentive to their situation.

For Memory and Meditation
"To sum up, all of you be harmonious, sympathetic, brotherly, kindhearted, and humble in spirit; not returning evil for evil or insult for insult, but giving a blessing instead." 1 Peter 3:8–9

Chapter 6
Persecution and Suffering
Focal Text: 1 Peter 3:13–22

Have you ever suffered or been persecuted because you were a Christian? Maybe you didn't get a job promotion because you don't drink or talk about the opposite sex in a demeaning sort of way—therefore, not fitting in and perhaps making others uncomfortable by the things you dion't do. Did you ever lose a friend because you defended or befriended someone outside of your social group? Or maybe you stood up for Christian values in a school board meeting or a city council and felt ostracized. Perhaps you did not even think about these things as suffering for the cross of Christ. You just did what you thought was right. And more than likely you had friends in your church family who loved and supported you.

Christians around the world, however, experience extreme suffering and persecution because they are Christ followers. Such was the case in Peter's day. Some believers were—and still are—alienated from their family and friends when they become believers. Christians in some parts of the world must worship in secret. And Christians in the first century as well as today continue to face imprisonment and even death because they choose to follow Christ.

We have seen that suffering is a major subject in 1 Peter. Although Peter has broached the topic previously in his letter, he doubles down on suffering at this point. There are parenthetic pauses addressing other matters, but suffering is a reoccurring theme throughout the remainder of the book.

Suffer for the Right Reason
1 Peter 3:13–17

Suffering is not always present in the life of the believer, but the potential for suffering in Jesus's name is always a real possibility. The question in verse 13 projects the believer to a future time of deliverance. Suffering is a constant threat in this life. Ultimately the pain of suffering will come to an end in the last days. No eternal harm will come to those who live for Jesus.

In verse 14, Peter turns to Isaiah 8 to remind God's people how Judah was threatened by aggressors. The northern kingdom of Israel and Assyria conspired to destroy Judah and her king. Judah was delivered exactly as God had said would happen. Peter wanted his readers to know that God will deliver the believer from persecution. Deliverance might not come immediately, but it will come. Suffering for righteousness brings a blessing from God. Peter was saying that believers have no reason to fear temporary suffering; they are assured of God's presence with them.

As a result of having confidence in God's sovereignty, the next step—verse 15—is to be ready to give a witness—even, and perhaps especially, in a time of suffering. Oppressors may bring persecution. The calm assurance (hope) of Jesus in our hearts empowers us to share the good news with those who oppress us. Our witness is to be sprinkled with grace toward those who mistreat us.

Then in verse 16, Peter alludes to social persecution. Christians at the time of Peter's letter were not experiencing widespread governmental persecution. Public shaming of Christians was practiced by nonbelievers—just as it seems to be in every age. These words are instructive to us. In our present setting we are experiencing the same type of oppression. We are to keep our conscience good toward God by continuing to live out our faith in the face of wrongful accusations. Some nonbelievers may come to Christ by observing our reactions to their taunts and sneers. In the last days all of the slanderers who do not come to Christ will themselves experience eternal shame.

Verse 17 tells us that it is God's sovereign will for some believers to suffer more than others. As mortals we find this inexplicable, beyond our human understanding. If God receives glory by allowing us to suffer for Him, it is to our benefit. No one or nothing can touch God's children without His permission. God allowed Satan to attack Job. The reason for individual suffering may not be apparent this side of heaven, but God will bring good for His kingdom out of believers' suffering. We must remember that our first parents in Eden were the ones who introduced sin and suffering into this world. Their actions have caused every generation to suffer. We life in a fallen universe, and suffering is one evidence of our state.

I have suffered for Jim. Sin has caused me to suffer. Bad choices have caused me to suffer. When I suffer at my own hand, I find it painful to bear. Suffering for Jesus, on the other hand, brings glory to God for the furtherance of the gospel. I have never regretted the little suffering I have experienced for Jesus's sake.

An Example of Christ's Suffering
1 Peter 3:18–22

Suffering is not an indication of Divine disfavor; actually the truth is to the contrary. Those who suffer for Jesus receive favor with the Father. Jesus is the prime example of the Father's favor. Jesus suffered while being righteous. He was vindicated by the Father at the resurrection. And Jesus set the example of a glorious resurrection to eternal life for all those who believe on His name.

The next section of Scripture is difficult to interpret. We may differ in how we look at the passage, but we can all agree that Jesus is ultimately triumphant over suffering and death. Because of His victory, we have the assurance that we too will be victorious over suffering and even death.

Verse 18 reminds us that Jesus died for sins once. He will never have to repeat His suffering. His suffering was unique. The suffering we experience in following Jesus is completely different from the suffering He experienced on our behalf. He died for our sins. He was sinless. He suffered and died for sinners. His death was substitutionary and vicarious. His death is the only avenue through which people can be made right with God. Jesus was put to death in the flesh, but He was raised by the power of the Holy Spirit. Romans 8:11 says: "But if the Spirit of Him who raised Jesus from the dead dwells in you, He who raised Christ Jesus from the dead will also give life to your mortal bodies through His Spirit who dwells in you." Those of us who have put our trust in Jesus's payment for our sins can rest in the assurance that we will one day share in His resurrection.

Scholars have various interpretations of verses 19–20a. Three of the four possible views can be reconciled with Scripture. The view that is out of bounds from biblical parameters is that Jesus went to hell in order to preach to people who had rejected Noah's preaching. This would mean that some or maybe all will have a second chance to be saved. Nowhere in the Word of God do we find this concept. To the contrary, the Bible says, "It is appointed for men to die once and after this comes judgment" (Heb. 9:27). To leave this life without Jesus is to seal one's eternal fate away from God. The Bible says nothing about second chances to be saved for anyone after this life on earth.

Another interpretation is that Christ preached through Noah to those who were in the prison of their sins. This means that Christ through the Spirit preached in Noah's day. This is a metaphorical approach to the passage, yet it is valid.

A third approach, which is held by many scholars, is that Jesus preached judgment to the spirits (fallen angels). These evil spirits were assigned to a designated place of punishment until the end time. In 2 Peter 2:4 a special word is used to describe the place of torment for the fallen angels. *Tartaroo* appears only once in the Greek manuscripts. These angels are those who rebelled against God during Noah's time. It would seem reasonable that Peter would refer twice to the confinement of the fallen angels. Jesus proclaimed His ultimate triumph over evil spirits when He visited them.

A fourth position, espoused by John Calvin, holds that Jesus preached to Old Testament saints who were prohibited from going into God's presence until the blood atonement had been made. Luke 16:19–31 describes the afterlife of two men. One of these men went to torment (hell), and the other departed this life and went to "Abraham's bosom" or the abode of the righteous dead. The entire underworld was referred to as "Hades." *Hades* is translated often simply as *hell* without distinguishing between the torment section and the abode of the righteous dead. When Jesus's Spirit preached to the Old Testament saints, He announced His victory at the cross. He emptied out the righteous side of Hades, taking them to heaven. Paul addressed this concept in his letter to the Ephesians: ""When He ascended on high, He led captive a host of captives, and He gave gifts to men" (Eph. 4:8).

Regardless of our thoughts on how to interpret this passage, the confidence we have is that to be absent from the body is to be present with the Lord (see 2 Cor. 5:8). In Philippians 1:23, the apostle Paul expressed his longing to "depart and be with Christ," adding, "For that is very much better." Because of the resurrection of Jesus, all saved people who die go immediately to be with the Lord.

Symbolism is apparent in verses 20b–21 in the correlation of the waters of Noah to the waters of baptism. Noah and his family were literally saved by the ark. Hebrews 11:7 says, "By faith Noah, being warned by God about things not yet seen, in reverence prepared an ark for the salvation of his household, by which he condemned the world, and became an heir of the righteousness which is according to faith." The fact that Noah was saved, along with his family, in the ark God led him to build—in spite of those who ridiculed him—vindicated his actions when judgment came on the unbelieving mockers at the flood. Noah's testimony was "saved" by the flood. Noah and his family were saved by the ark with the water setting them apart from those who perished in the world.

Baptism is the first step of obedience of the believer. After Jesus's ascension and the coming of the Holy Spirit, Peter preached, "Repent, and each of you be baptized in the name of Jesus Christ for the forgiveness of your sins; and you will receive the gift of the Holy Spirit" (Acts 2:38). Baptism does not cleanse a person from his or her sins. Baptism does not appropriate grace. Baptism is like Noah's floodwaters. Baptism shows that the believer is set apart from the world to the glory of God. With a clear conscience the believer knows his or her obedience is an expression of confidence in the power of God. Jesus is our ark!

As this chapter draws to a close, we once again are brought back to victory in Jesus. The power of Jesus's resurrection places Him at the right hand of the Father. We see the ultimate authority Jesus has over the evil spirits. Because of Jesus, we can win in this life over suffering and evil. Because of Jesus, we will eternally overcome suffering and death. He is our example through all of life's trials. And His presence will see us through all suffering and persecution.

For Memory and Meditation
"But sanctify Christ as Lord in your hearts, always being ready to make a defense to everyone who asks you to give an account for the hope that is in you, yet with gentleness and reverence." 1 Peter 3:15

Chapter 7
Choosing to Suffer
Focal Text: 1 Peter 4:1–19

For anyone to choose suffering may sound strange. You've got to wonder what the options are for a person to choose to suffer. Many people believe that decisions are based on some sort of reward. Choosing to eat cake when you really shouldn't is a decision based on memories of how good that cake tastes. Choosing to exercise, even if you don't like it, is based on the benefits you know you'll receive. Choosing to help a person in need may be based on the accolades you think you'll receive because of your good deed or sincerely because of the good feeling you get by being of service to another person created in the image of God. But suffering? Who chooses that?

By observing Christ's suffering, Peter saw believers who accepted ridicule. These believers had decided to refuse sin's dominance. The apostle reminded his readers that at one time they had lived like the unsaved. Now those in the world were persecuting them because the believers would no longer participate in the old lifestyle. The end result is that those who have chosen to follow Christ will be vindicated in the judgment. God will set all things right in the last day.

Fervent Love
1 Peter 4:1–9

Prepared to Suffer (4:1–2)
The use of the word "therefore" in the first verse of chapter 4 points us back to the previous section of Scripture that describes Jesus's victory over suffering and death. Believers who suffer can be assured they will receive a reward that will last for eternity.

The words "arm yourselves" in verse 1 suggest an allusion to military readiness, preparedness, ready to face whatever threat may come. With determination and discipline a believer is to be prepared to suffer for the gospel. Jesus suffered physically, emotionally, and spiritually. We can expect the same treatment He received so Peter tells us to be ready.

God may allow some believers to suffer in order to further the gospel. Have you ever known people who bore suffering from poor health with utmost Christian grace? Their witness of their love for Christ in the midst of their pain and impairments is a testimony that truly inspires. Imagine how often God has used such a witness to get the attention of unbelievers.

Most scholars think Paul's suffering described in 2 Corinthians 12:7–10 was some type of physical malady. Sometimes sickness is a result of living in a sin-cursed world. All the children of Adam suffer from a common curse. This is why we get sick and eventually die. Thanks be unto God that Jesus is the one and only ultimate cure.

The last phrase of verse 1 is a challenge to understand. Some people teach that believers can reach a state of sinless perfection. This is not the meaning here or anywhere else in Scripture. But it does show how believers who have prepared themselves to suffer for the gospel have broken from the old lifestyle of sinfulness. In itself this choice sets the believer apart from the lifestyle of the unbeliever.

Verse 2 is an admonition for believers to live out their lives in the will of God. Life is too short to waste it on selfish lusts. We will be spending an eternity with Jesus. Whatever time we have remaining in life should be lived for our Lord.

Separated for God (4:3–5)

The word *Gentiles* in our English Bibles comes from the Greek word *ethne*. Peter was describing the people of the world as separate from the people of God. He said some of those who had been saved used to swim in a pool of sin. New Testament writers include a number of lists of specific sins believers are to avoid. Among the passages dealing with these sins are Romans 13:13; 1 Corinthians 5:10–11; 6:9–10; and Galatians 5:19–21, to name only a few as examples Paul provided.

All five of the examples from Paul's lists of sins include drunkenness. Drinking parties provided an occasion for sexual sins and other types of illicit behavior. So many of the other sins listed might be associated with drinking alcoholic beverages.

I continue to be amazed at how many believers maintain that alcohol consumption is acceptable as a liberty found in Christ. While the Greek word *oinophlygia* occurs only once in the New Testament, this word for drunkenness has become the cover for those who want to drink socially. Some ministers of the gospel will even argue for the use of alcohol as a beverage on the basis that only drunkenness is sin. The English word *carousing* comes from the Greek word *potoi*, which refers to social drinking parties that provided opportunity to plunge into debased activities. After coming to Christ, believers were to stay away from such activities. Believers are to abstain from all appearance of evil (see 1 Thess. 5:22).

Peter's reference to idolatry denotes that the recipients of his letter were Gentiles rather than Jews. The observant Jew would not have been involved in the type of practices found at the social drinking parties. Veneration of the emperor was a part of the public parties. Worshipping an idol came easily in such settings.

The pagans were surprised that the new believers would no longer engage in what was considered normal cultural activities. Criticism came on believers because they were social misfits. When I came to Christ, I lost all my so-called friends, but God gave me multiplied numbers of brothers and sisters in Christ to replace them. That's one way brothers and sisters in Christ, fellowshipping together through a church, can support one another. And who has more fun than a bunch of Christians? Alcohol is not needed for fun Christian fellowship.

Governmental persecution would come to believers soon, but many biblical historians think that at the time of

Peter's letter believers were not experiencing a systematic crackdown on Christianity. Believers were, however, social outcasts because they were out of step with the popular cultural norms. Eventually physical persecution and even death would come.

Christians in the United States enjoyed preferential treatment for over two hundred years. The winds of social change have brought about a castigation of the faithful. Whether the issue is religious liberty or the normalization of homosexuality, believers find themselves on the outside of power and influence. Being socially ostracized for biblical convictions is the forerunner of more severe persecution.

Peter reminds us to take the long look. God's judgment will rectify all wrongs. We are not to seek revenge or even to desire retribution for those who oppose the things of God. We are to seek their conversion. In the last days those who choose to oppose God and His people will answer to a greater final authority.

The Purpose of the Gospel (4:6)

Some who had trusted Christ had died. The unbelievers were mocking the faithful by saying there was no difference between believer and nonbeliever. The charge was that everyone is going to taste death; therefore, everyone should live fully for this life.

Peter pointed out once again that the gospel gives eternal life. Those who reject the gospel do not get the final word. The rich and famous unbelievers lauded by culture will stand before the ultimate judge. The believer will live on forever with God.

Suffering according to the Will of God
1 Peter 4:12–19

I have preached the funerals of babies. I have watched people waste away in the prime of life with cancer. All kinds of human suffering that comes as a result of wars, famine, natural disasters, and terrorism cause us to ask, "Why do people suffer?" I do not have all the answers. I can share with you from God's Word some explanations about suffering. God uses suffering to cause believers to turn from sin. When we experience suffering—our own or what we observe in others, we either run to God, or we run from God. We have nowhere else to turn when suffering comes. We must turn to the Lord. When that happens, we turn away from sin.

God is sovereign. No suffering can come our way that God does not permit. Believers will stand before the judgment seat of Christ. Suffering can purify us for that moment. If believers are saved by grace, where will the ungodly stand in the judgment on the last day? This is all the more reason to trust a Creator that He will work all things for our good and for His glory.

The Inevitability of Suffering (4:12)

Suffering and trials are not out of the ordinary. Adam brought sin into the world, and death entered the world because of that first sin. Trouble comes our way because we are a part of the human race (see Job 5:7). Life itself ensures suffering.

The words *testing* and *trials* come from the same root word. *Test* comes from the Greek word *peirasmon*, and *trials* translates the word *peirasmois* used in 1 Peter 1:6. Suffering should not come as a surprise to us. Suffering is not an act of capricious fate but is a normal experience for the believer.

The Investment of Suffering (4:13)

Suffering will eventually pay dividends here and hereafter. No one likes to suffer. A mentally challenged child, a dreaded or prolonged disease, or the loss of a loved one are all heartbreaking. God paints a silver lining in every cloud with Romans 8:28–29: "And we know that God causes all things to work together for good to those who love God, to those who are called according to His purpose. For those whom He foreknew, He also predestined to become conformed to the image of His Son, so that He would be the firstborn among many brethren." God's purpose is to make us like Jesus.

God sometimes uses unpleasant experiences to mold us. The difficulties of life will happen. God uses them to help us. Romans 8:18 tells us that in heaven the glory of Christ will reveal the benefits of the suffering that we rightfully endured on earth. By rejoicing during our suffering, we show that we truly are followers of Jesus. Jesus said that we are to rejoice when we are persecuted (see Matt. 5:12). Rejoicing gives a testimony of our faith in a just God.

Innocently Suffering (4:14–16)

Suffering can come because of our own sin. Some sow wild oats and pray for a crop failure. Reaping wild oats is an unpleasant harvest. We are to suffer for the Savior, not self. Suffering the consequences of our own sins offers no benefit or reward. We neither glorify God nor grow closer to Him when we suffer because of our sin.

The list of sins is only a sampling for consideration. Most Christians would not participate in the sins listed, but being a "troublesome meddler" might be a trap for even the dedicated believer. Interestingly, the Greek word for "troublesome meddler," *allotriepiskopos*, appears only once in the New Testament. For that matter, the word cannot be found in any other Greek writings of the time.

The bottom line here is that Christians are to refrain from any activity that might bring suffering to oneself or others. Remember the little chant we were taught when we were kids, "Sticks and stones may break my bones, but words will never hurt me." I suppose children learn those words to try to brush off the sting of hurtful insults. As we get older, we know with certainly that words cause suffering and leave scars just as much as a physical wound. James instructed us to bridle our tongues (Jas. 3). Christians ought not cause others to suffer, even suffering that comes from unkind words.

You have heard people say, "I can't understand why that person has to suffer; she hasn't done anything wrong." Other than learning to avoid the sin, there is little or no benefit in suffering for our own foolish choices. Suffering should be to the glory of God.

Intent of Suffering (4:17–18)
If judgment begins with the people of God and they barely escape, what will be the fate of those without Christ? God loves His children. He wants what is best for them. For those who are disobedient to the gospel, only a final judgment awaits them regardless of the earthly suffering they experience. Peter alludes to the great white throne judgment that awaits unbelievers.

Peter restates in proverbial form his observation of judgment contrasting the household of God and the disobedient. The righteous are barely saved. Suffering authenticates saving faith. Suffering shows that believers are not immune from the same trials lost people face. It gives us the opportunity to show we can react differently from the world. Trials come our way to prove what we are made of.

The last explanation about suffering found in the text shows that suffering can also be intentional.

Intentional Suffering (4:19)
God is sovereign. This means God is in control of all things. By His decrees we are born, live, and die. Jesus said not one

sparrow would fall that the Father does not know about. God is the Creator; therefore, He is sovereign over all of His creation's affairs (see Ps. 115:3). God is not some passive observer but rather a loving Father who watches over His children with the greatest of compassions. When suffering comes our way, we still may not understand why we are facing such hardships. God allows us to see some things here, but usually such understanding will not be revealed until we get to heaven; that is what faith is all about.

Suffering is an inconvenience of this world, which will soon be past. We have encouraging words for difficult days!

Being a Living Witness in a Dying World
1 Peter 4:7–11

As an interlude between two sections of Scripture that directly deal with suffering, the apostle calls the Christian to a consistently faithful life. Regardless of whether persecution is present, the believer has the responsibility to live a godly life. The purpose of life itself is to bring glory to God through Jesus Christ.

Last Days (4:7)
The last days began after the ascension of Jesus into heaven. It has been almost two thousand years since Jesus left, but His return is certain. Nevertheless, His return is imminent. We are not to set dates for His coming. We are not to live in cloistered compounds waiting for a cataclysmic end of this

world. Because Jesus could come at any moment, we should be stimulated to action. Our lives count greatly when we help others in the body of Christ. We are to be a living witness to a dying world. Ultimately we glorify God through Jesus Christ.

The end time does not require us to perform extraordinary feats. We are simply to live our lives according to spiritual purposes. Prayer is a primary function to exhibit a spiritual purpose. Whatever gets accomplished in this life depends on the power of God through prayer.

Love and the Believer (4:8–9)

Love is the birthmark of the believer in Christ. Jesus said this would be the way those outside the family of God would know we are His disciples (see John 13:35). Love does not come naturally to us. It must be Holy Spirit infused. Fervent love comes by way of working at loving people by a supernatural enablement.

"Love covers a multitude of sins" means that when we love our brothers and sisters in Christ, we will not hold a grudge or seek retaliation. Hatred motivates a person to seek to harm those who have sinned. This is not to excuse sin. Love will help draw the errant one back into fellowship. People need love.

The early Christians practiced hospitality. Lodging was expensive for the first-century traveler. Bed and board were difficult to secure. Believers opened their homes to other believers. This accelerated gospel advance in the Roman world. At times, demands may have been wearisome for the hosts. Believers were to see their hospitality as a service to the Lord.

Gifted Believers (4:10–11)

The word "gift" is the Greek word *charisma*. God graciously supplies at least one gift to every believer. Since the ability to honor God is a gift, no one can boast. Bragging about a gift would contradict God's gracious character in bestowing the gift.

Building up others in the faith is the primary function of the gifts. As stewards we should realize that the gifts do not belong to us. We are managers of our gifts. Gifts are to be used responsibly by a manager. We are to use the gift as the Master intended.

Peter divides the gifts into two expressions, speaking and serving. The apostle Paul goes into detail about various gifts, but essentially all gifts listed in the New Testament fall into one of these two expressions. Peter gives us a general listing rather than going into specifics.

When God's gifts are expressed, they must be used according to the Word of God. Speaking the "utterances of God" is not bringing new revelation to be added to Scripture. Some modern-day religious groups believe God expands His revelation by giving special wording to them. God speaks in and through His written Word. A speaking ministry must be based on the revealed Word of God found in our Bible. When serving, we must use our gifts in the power of the Spirit. He supplies the strength for us to do the work God wants us to do.

All of the speaking and serving are to bring glory to God through Jesus Christ. Peter closes this section of his writing with a doxology. It is not an end to his writing but a shift in emphasis once again back to the theme of suffering. The "amen" is an affirmation that all proceeding is true.

For Memory and Meditation
"Whoever speaks, is to do so as one who is speaking the utterances of God; whoever serves is to do so as one who is serving by the strength which God supplies; so that in all things God may be glorified through Jesus Christ, to whom belongs the glory and dominion forever and ever." 1 Peter 4:11

Chapter 8
Final Words of Insight
1 Peter 5:1-14

Except for one brief mention in chapter 5, suffering is no longer the focus in the apostle Peter's first letter. Peter now turns his attention to the church. He gives a brief directive to the leaders. He encourages younger men to follow the leadership of the elders. Peter points out the power of humility and warns about the reality of spiritual warfare. He reminds the recipients of his letter about difficult days that are overcome by an all-powerful God. Peter concludes with some personal remarks.

Expectations of Spiritual Leadership
1 Peter 5:1–5a

Instructions to the Elders (5:1)

Peter speaks to the elders of the church. The word "elders" comes from the Greek word *presbyteroi*. Three words are used to describe the person or persons providing leadership to the church—elder, pastor (*poimaino*), and overseer (*episkopountes*). The Greek words are different, but their function and office in the New Testament church are often interchangeable. The pastor intimates the role of a shepherd. He is the one who takes care of the flock. The overseer is one who seeks to provide oversight of the direction of the church. Elders are those who minister in the Word to the body of believers.

Some believe that every church should have a plurality of elders. While it is possible this is the desired norm, some churches are too small or full of new converts that would make it impossible to have a plurality of elders. Others believe that elders form a decision-making body apart from the congregation. In this case the congregation abdicates authority to a ruling group. Peter considered himself a "fellow elder" although he was an apostle. There are leaders among peers. Elders were likely men who had a role as overseer that rose to the top of the group. Second, the congregations described in the New Testament never forfeited their responsibility before God to a group of leaders.

Peter laid claim to having observed the sufferings of Jesus and to having viewed the glory to come. Perhaps Peter was referring to the Mount of Transfiguration when he saw the glorified Christ. Maybe he was talking about the resurrection when he saw the risen Lord. No doubt Peter was looking for a better day.

Tasks for the Elders (5:2–3)
Specific tasks of the elders were explained with prohibitions listed as well in these two verses. A person answers the call of God to minister voluntarily. No one should be a

pastor or elder who seeks the work as a job. Financial gain is never to be the motivating factor in serving as a pastor. Basically the two pitfalls that destroy a man of ministry are sexual indiscretion and financial impropriety. Usually hubris precedes any fall of a minister. Peter gives caution about this temptation a few verses later.

Leaders cannot demand people to follow them. They must earn people's trust before people will follow their lead. When someone has to say he is in charge, then he probably is not. Ministers cannot force people into compliance. Even if the desire is to see positive results for the kingdom, people must voluntarily seek to serve the Lord. Leadership by example is a minister's best approach.

The Crown of Glory (5:4)

Peter refers to Jesus as "the Chief Shepherd." This title is found nowhere else in the New Testament. This is a reminder to readers in the early church as well as today that the church belongs to Jesus—not to church leaders or members. Those who minister do so under the lordship of Jesus Christ. Decisions that are made in the local church are not to be made by one man or any group's preferences. The direction of the church should be set out by the Spirit of God through the Word of God.

Faithful pastors will receive a crown. In the Roman world a crown of leaves was given to the winner of a game or a victor of a battle. The pastor will receive a crown that is unfading. It will never wilt or wither away.

Five crowns are mentioned in the New Testament. "The crown of righteousness" is awarded to those who look for the appearing of Jesus (see 2 Tim. 4:8). The incorruptible crown (see 1 Cor. 9:25–27) is given to those who finish faithfully. James 1:12 speaks of "the crown of life." This crown is for the faithful believer who endures trials. The crown of rejoicing is for the believer who has been a winner of the lost (see 1 Thess. 2:19). Anyone can win any of these crowns. But only a faithful pastor can receive "the crown of glory."

The Role of the Younger Men (5:5a)

Younger men were to submit to the leadership of the elders. All elders are not advanced in age, but they were chosen because of their spiritual maturity. Most younger men need to mature in their decision-making process before assuming a leadership role. The best way for this to happen is for elders to mentor younger men. The key to success is when younger men are willing to submit to elders.

Engaging in Spiritual Warfare
1 Peter 5:5b–9

The greatest threat to gospel advance is pride. Pride was Satan's downfall (see Isa. 14). Arrogance caused Adam and Eve to sin in the garden of Eden. Almost every sin can be traced to the cancer of pride. We can depend on only one way to ensure victory in spiritual warfare. Humility before God unleashes His power in our lives. We are no longer depending on self-effort. We are depending on the Spirit's work.

Clothed with Humility (5:5b–6)
When the verse says "all of you," that means me; that means you. Peter uses Proverbs 3:34 to emphasize the imperative of humility: "Though He scoffs at the scoffers, yet He gives grace to the afflicted."

Jesus used a story to tell how a person should view himself (see Luke 14:7–11). He said it is better to be lifted up to the head table than to be embarrassed by having to go to the back of the room. Jesus said those who exalt themselves will be humbled. Those who are humble will be exalted. The "proper time" referred to in the text alludes to the last days.

Both James and 1 Peter mention humility and resisting the devil. Those were common themes in the early church. The two writers had different audiences. James was calling complacent believers to faithfulness, while Peter was encouraging believers who were suffering for the gospel.

No Need to Worry (5:7)
I have often quoted this verse to encourage people to trust in the Lord during some period of challenge. Some commentators see anxiety or cares as akin to pride. They would see this statement as more of a rebuke than a consolation. Either way, there is only One we can trust with our trials. He always cares for us.

Stay Alert (5:8–9)

Believers are to be on the watch for a spiritual adversary who will do anything possible to destroy our testimony. Satan is not a force. He is a real being. He is a fallen celestial creature with extraordinary power. He is powerful but not all powerful. His roar is more ferocious than his bite. Only God is all powerful.

One of Satan's roaring tactics is fear. If he can cause you to fear the future, fear suffering, fear the consequences of your actions, or any number of other things, he wins. We have a promise from God that "perfect love casts out fear" (1 John 4:18). Whatever the devil does is ineffective when we are aware of his efforts. Believers everywhere see the will of God accomplished when they refuse to fall prey to the roaring lion.

Exiting with Spiritual Promises
1 Peter 5:10–14

Peter's entire letter is capsuled in verse 10. He sums up his writings about suffering and the promises of God. He quickly moves to a doxology of praise. The concluding remarks are personal in nature following the typical end of a first-century letter.

Closing Confidence and Encouragement (5:10–11)

Peter says that suffering will last only for a "little" time. In the human context we see people suffer. From the eternal perspective time is of no real consequence. When the believer gets to heaven, earthly sufferings will not even be a faint memory. The glory revealed in heaven far outweighs any suffering we endure in this life. In 2 Corinthians 4:16–18, Paul wrote: "Therefore we do not lose heart, but though our outer man is decaying, yet our inner man is being renewed day by day. For momentary, light affliction is producing for us an eternal weight of glory far beyond all comparison, while we look not at the things which are seen, but at the things which are not seen; for the things which are seen are temporal, but the things which are not seen are eternal."

God gives His promise that He will "perfect, confirm, strengthen and establish" us in the last days. "For I am confident of this very thing, that He who began a good work in you will perfect it until the day of Christ Jesus" (Phil. 1:6). What God starts, He finishes. If He initiated a work of grace in you, He will see that you persevere to the end of this life.

The song of praise emphasizes the power of God. Even when He permits His children to suffer or allows the devil to disrupt lives, God is still in firm control of time and eternity. When Peter said, "Amen," he was affirming all that had been said before and looking for the fulfillment of all the promises.

In Closing (5:12–14)

Silvanus could possibly be Silas, who was one of Paul's frequent companions. More than likely Silvanus was not Silas. A second issue arises about whether Silvanus was Peter's amanuensis or the one commissioned to carry the letter to the churches. Even if Silvanus penned the words, Peter was the author of the words. If Peter used Silvanus as a secretary, the Holy Spirit used Peter to convey the words.

Peter gave one last charge to his readers. He wanted them to stand firm in the truth.

Greetings and a benediction include a reference to an unnamed woman in Babylon. Churches in the New Testament are referred to in the feminine gender (for examples, see 2 Cor. 11:2; Eph. 5:22–33; Rev. 19:7–9; and 2 John). It is highly probable that the lady mentioned in verse 1 Peter 5:13 is a church.

The location of the church to whom Peter is writing is in Babylon. The Babylon of the Old Testament was in ruins. It was no longer a population center. Some think Peter's reference here is to Rome. The Babylon of the book of Revelation is considered to be Rome. This would put Peter in Rome. There is no evidence that he ever went to Rome. It is likely that Peter was using the term "Babylon" in the sense that the people of God are in exile in this world. We are in a strange and harsh land. Praise God, we have the comfort and the assurance to know that He is with us and will never leave us.

John Mark accompanied Paul on his first missionary journey. Mark abandoned the mission causing a rift between Paul and Barnabas. Apparently, Mark was brought back to a place of trustworthiness. Paul spoke highly of Mark (see 2 Tim. 4:11). Peter had a long-standing relationship with Mark. The early church had met in the home of Mark's mother (see Acts 12:12). Peter considered Mark his son in the ministry. Some believe that Mark's Gospel was augmented by Peter.

Peter encouraged a show of love among the church members. He prayed a blessing of peace over them. Peter knew that being in Christ transcended any suffering we find in this life. Peter offered encouraging words for difficult days.

For Memory and Meditation
"Therefore humble yourselves under the mighty hand of God, that He may exalt you at the proper time, casting all your anxiety on Him, because He cares for you." 1 Peter 5:6

Introduction to 2 Peter

In his first letter Peter repeatedly addressed the issue of suffering. In his second letter Peter talked about faith in the midst of false teachers as the last days approach. Christians faced difficulties in the first century from within and without. False teachers had already begun to create problems for the early church. Peter continued to offer encouraging words for difficult days.

The book of 2 Peter is so named for two reasons: First, Peter is the self-proclaimed writer, announcing that this is the case in 2 Peter 3:1. Second, 2 Peter is the only New Testament book not quoted by church leaders for the first three hundred years. Yet this letter became an important part of the canonized Word of God.

Christianity was life and death for believers in the apostolic age. Peter still had to challenge the church to grow to maturity and to remain doctrinally pure. In many parts of the world, people are still putting their lives on the line when they publicly profess Jesus. In the United States we are not threatened with death, but many experience negative repercussions when seeking to live out their faith.

In what was probably Peter's last communication, he reduced life down to the bare minimum: know you are saved and live like it. We find some pertinent information in chapter 1 about making sure we have a relationship with God.

Chapter 9
Faith That Is Sure
Focal Text: 2 Peter 1:1–21

Some Christians doubt their salvation from time to time. It is unfortunate and unnecessary, but it happens. Maybe a person accepted Christ at a young age and, looking back, wonders whether she really knew what she was doing at that time. Or perhaps someone has committed a sin that continues to interrupt his sleep; he has asked God to forgive him—and believes He has—but he keeps thinking about what he has done. And he wonders if anyone like him can really enter heaven's gates. Then, maybe, a believer reads God's Word about what Christians should be like—what they should do and not do. She knows she falls far short. Can someone like her really be saved?

Believers should have no higher priority than to be sure of where they will spend eternity. The apostle Peter told the early Christians to be sure of their relationship with God. Jesus provides salvation, perpetuates salvation, and concludes salvation.

Peter was an unlettered man. He became schooled at the feet of Jesus. Peter sets forth the way to have full assurance of eternal life. Those who profess to know the Lord are encouraged to be sure of their faith. Making sure we have a valid conversion is the first step in knowing we have eternal life.

God working in our lives reassures us that we have a relationship with Him..

Greetings
2 Peter 1:1–2

Peter, as the author of this book, is writing to those who have been saved by the righteousness of Jesus Christ. He proclaims Jesus as God. Peter's opening greeting is common to first-century Christian letters. He expresses a desire for the recipients to have grace and peace. Grace always comes before peace. People will have no peace without first experiencing the grace of God in Jesus Christ. The world clamors for peace, but the only basis for true peace is the grace of God.

Born from Above
2 Peter 1:3–4

In John 3:3, Jesus spoke of being born again or born from above. We have characteristics like our Heavenly Father and spiritual brother, Jesus, when we become "partakers of the divine nature." We are born into the family of God.

Conversion takes place at a point in time. I had a seminary professor who said that you can be saved and not know when it happened. Salvation is not obtained by holy osmosis. When Jesus comes into your life, you will know it. Becoming a follower of Jesus and not knowing it would be like getting married and not knowing it. You may not remember the date on the calendar or the time on the clock, but you will be cognizant of the decision you made to receive Jesus.

Saving grace is the divine supernatural infusion of God's person into the life of the believer. This can only happen by the power of God. He calls us unto Himself. We are never sinless this side of heaven, but His divine presence in us never sins. John wrote, "No one who is born of God practices sin, because His seed abides in him; and he cannot sin, because he is born of God" (1 John 3:9). We can resist the allure of sin because of the power of God within us.

Grow Up
2 Peter 1:5–11

Physical growth requires a proper diet. Spiritual growth is no different. Spiritual growth requires a special diet. The new believer starts with the milk of God's Word (see 1 Pet. 2:2), eventually moving to the meat (see Heb. 5:14). Growth toward spiritual maturity continues until we see Jesus. Spiritual growth is an expectation of every believer (see 2 Pet. 3:18).

Any spiritual growth a believer experiences is enabled by God. This growth shows the evidence of grace. When a professing Christian is not experiencing spiritual growth, the lack of growing discipleship is an indication that something is wrong (see Luke 13:6–9). Sadly, some who are "partakers of the Divine nature" have not added to their faith. They have failed to grow properly. Because of their lack of spiritual maturity, they are susceptible to doubting their salvation. A second reason for a child of God to doubt his salvation is hidden sin (see Ps. 66:18).

Uncertainty about salvation is common but unnecessary. Believers who are doubting their salvation should confess all known sin and grow spiritually to enjoy the Lord's reassuring presence. God is the One who begins the work of salvation. He is the One who provides the strength to finish the journey of faith (see Phil. 1:6; 2:13; 1 Thess. 5:24).

Reminder
2 Peter 1:12–15

Stories of endurance inspire us. We are encouraged when we hear about those who have overcome adversity. Yet it is the daily grind, the everyday doing what we must do, that pays off in the long run. Few people see the sacrifice and labor in the prayer closet or ministering in an obscure place.

Peter wanted to impress upon his readers eternal truth. He had instructed them previously in his first letter. Now Peter was saying we never get to the point when we do not need to be reminded of the basics.

Verse 12 is a reminder of the presence of the truth. Jesus is the ultimate truth. In John's Gospel (14:6), Jesus said, "I am the way, and the truth, and the life; no one comes to the Father but through Me." The Word of God is perfect truth; again John wrote (John 17:17): "Sanctify them in the truth;

Your word is truth." The truth we know about Jesus we get from the Scriptures. We are to base our beliefs on the Word of God. Experiences can be false. The written Word of God has no flaws.

Peter knew his time on earth was drawing to a close. He had received a special revelation from Jesus that his life was about to end. He wanted to use his remaining days to call his friends to a deeper walk with the Lord.

According to tradition the apostles were martyred for Jesus. Peter knew soon there would be no eyewitness of the life of Christ. Peter affirmed that the eternal Word of God would remain. The Scriptures give testimony to the work of God. Those who have gone before us still bear testimony in many ways. The writer of Hebrews stated this well: "Therefore, since we have so great a cloud of witnesses surrounding us, let us also lay aside every encumbrance and the sin which so easily entangles us, and let us run with endurance the race that is set before us, fixing our eyes on Jesus, the author and perfecter of faith, who for the joy set before Him endured the cross, despising the shame, and has sat down at the right hand of the throne of God" (12:1–2).

A Sure Word of Prophesy
2 Peter 1:16-21

The apostles had a unique privilege to see Jesus during His journey on this earth. In Acts 1 we find one of the qualifications for an apostle was to be an eyewitness of the resurrection of Jesus. John wrote about how he had touched the Lord Jesus physically. When Peter spoke of seeing Jesus in His majesty, this was likely a reference to the Mount of Transfiguration event found in Matthew 17. Personal experience is powerful. Prophetic revelation is even more convincing. Peter cited prophecy as the ultimate evidence for Jesus's being the Lord and Savior. Peter said there was a sure Word of God.

The word "prophecy" in the Bible has two different elements: forth-telling, proclaiming the truth of God, and fore-telling, prophesying a future event. Someone has said that two-thirds of the Scriptures are prophetic, and one-half of all prophecy is yet to be fulfilled. The test for a prophet of God is found in Deuteronomy 18:19–22. God's prophecy will always be 100 percent true.

Studying the future has a certain fascination and excitement. It stirs the emotions and captivates the mind. Palm readers, psychics, and those who are involved with the occult capitalize on anxiety about the future. Success of apocalyptic movies shows public interest in the future. Christian films usually fail to capture with quality the reality of the end time. When we invoke the word *prophecy*, some become excited while others roll their eyes.

Jesus is the person of prophecy. Every book of the Bible testifies of Jesus. Every text of Scripture leads you to the Lord Jesus. He is the subject of the Book.

God revealed to Adam that a Savior was coming (see Gen. 3:14–15). Abraham was told that Christ would be from his lineage (see Gen. 12:1–3). Jacob understood that the Messiah would come from the tribe of Judah (see Gen. 49:10). David received the promise that the Christ would rule on his throne (see 2 Sam. 7: 12–13). Isaiah saw Christ as the Suffering Servant (see Isa. 53). Micah revealed Christ's birthplace of Bethlehem (see Mic. 5:2). Zechariah tells that the Christ would be betrayed for thirty pieces of silver (see Zech. 11:13). The psalmist pictures Christ crucified and resurrected (see Pss. 22:16; 16:10–11). More than one hundred biblical prophecies were literally fulfilled at Jesus's first coming. Jesus used the Old Testament prophecies to convince the Emmaus Road disciples that He was the Christ (see Luke 24:44).

Many in our culture might scoff at the belief in a totally true and trustworthy Bible. Fulfilled prophecy answers this criticism. The Bible is not only up-to-date; it is far ahead of today's date. The Word of God, prophecy in particular, points to Jesus as Lord and Savior.

In his book *Expository Sermons on the Epistles of Peter* (Zondervan, 1982), Dr. W. A. Criswell commented on these verses, "What Peter saw with his eyes and what he heard with his ears does not equal the affirmation of the glory and the deity of Christ that is presented in the Word of God." It is astonishing the apostle writes that the Word of God is a better revelation than his own eyewitness.

Verse 19 points us to Jesus. He is the morning star. His light shines into our lives through the good news (see 2 Cor. 4:4).

The last two verses of 2 Peter 1 give us once again the confirmation that the Bible is a word from God. The Bible always leads you right, and it contains no errors. During a pastorate years ago, I was in a meeting with church leaders that became focused on one of the traditional practices of the church. I pointed out the Scriptures were clear in prohibiting the practice. One of the more vocal members of the group spoke up and said, "I don't care what the Bible says. We are going to do it anyway." Thankfully other church leaders in that meeting were courageous enough to stand with the scriptural teaching. What the Bible says takes precedent over any other opinion.

We must base the entirety of our lives on the teachings from God's Word. God used men to pen His Word, but the Holy Spirit protected them from error. Forty men wrote sixty-six books in at least three languages over a span of fifteen hundred years. One central truth brings the books into perfect unity, God's glory revealed in Jesus Christ. The Bible is an enduring, eternal Word from God.

The word "interpretation," recorded in verse 20, comes from a Greek word that means "origin." Eternal truth comes from God, not man. The Word was breathed out by God. "All Scripture is inspired by God and profitable for teaching, for reproof, for correction, for training in righteousness" (2 Tim. 3:16). The Word was transmitted by God. The Bible came dynamically through men providing plenary, verbal, errorless truth.

People can discover many truths, but spiritual truth can only be revealed by God. A prominent former pastor and denominational employee in Texas wrote a theological paper entitled "The Errancy of Inerrancy." He claimed the Bible was sufficient in matters of faith but contained errors when it spoke in the areas of science or history. Contrary to his claim, God can reveal only errorless truth (see Titus 1:2; Heb. 6:18).

Have you considered the total truthful testimony of the Word of God about Jesus? Have you come to a place in your life where you have received him as your Lord and Savior? If not, you can right now. Give your life to Him as the risen Lord and trust Him as the blood payment for your eternal forgiveness of sin. Ask Him to come into your life. He will do it.

For Memory and Meditation
"Therefore, brethren, be all the more diligent to make certain about His calling and choosing you; for as long as you practice these things, you will never stumble; for in this way the entrance into the eternal kingdom of our Lord and Savior Jesus Christ will be abundantly supplied to you." 2 Peter 1:10–11

Chapter 10
False Teachers That Are Real
Focal Text: 2 Peter 2:1–22

Peter warned the early believers about false teachers. False teaching destroys the true witness of the gospel. Peter wanted the believers to realize false teachers would destroy their walk with God. Christians are still in danger of false teachers. More derivatives of Christianity have emerged in the last 150 years than in the previous nineteen hundred years. False teaching is not new. Paul faced legalists. Jude took on those who undermined the message of the gospel. Peter warned those who denied a future judgment.

In our day we have theologians who espouse the Openness of God Theory. They say God is unable to see all the future. According to their belief, God was caught off guard when the Twin Towers went down in New York City. The Openness Theory supposedly absolves God of His prior knowledge of evil. One Scripture passage that refutes the Openness of God theory is Isaiah 46:9–11. Isaiah wrote: "Remember the former things long past, for I am God, and there is no other; I am God, and there is no one like Me, declaring the end from the beginning, and from ancient times things which have not been done, saying, 'My purpose will be established, and I will accomplish all My good pleasure.' . . .

Truly I have spoken; truly I will bring it to pass. I have planned it, surely I will do it."

To say God is unaware of future events or human actions is to deny His sovereignty. This is one example of a myriad of theological aberrations foisted upon people.

So-called ministers teach that God wants everyone to be wealthy. Some say God wants everyone to be healed from their diseases. Sadly, false doctrine usually is accompanied by a failing morality. Generally ministers fall because of girls, gold, or glory. False teaching and failing morality are often coupled together.

Scholars point out a striking similarity between 2 Peter 2 and the book of Jude. Liberal scholars, a term that is almost an oxymoron, say that neither letter was written during the time of the apostles. Obviously, 2 Peter 2 and Jude include strikingly similar words. Some suggest that one of the writers borrowed from the other. All theories aside, we can be confident that both Peter and Jude were saying, "Don't be fooled!" Four facts relating to false teachers can be clearly seen in this chapter.

Purveyors of Falsehood
2 Peter 2:1–3a

Satan's supersalesmen are everywhere. Religion is a profitable market. People get uncomfortable when you begin to point out that Mormonism, Jehovah's Witnesses, Oneness

Pentecostalism, or some other aberrant form of Christianity is in error. False teachers use their tongues to deceive.

Sometimes a robbery will be committed with the help of someone on the inside of a business. We call it an inside job. Jude 4 speaks of the false teachers on the inside of the church. False teachers inside the church steal the truth away from God's people. The Lord Jesus paid for the false teachers' redemption, but by their false doctrines they have denied Him.

Verse 2 says that the false teachers lead many away from the truth. Speaking against the true gospel, the false teachers propagate an alternate gospel. Romans 1:25 speaks of exchanging the truth for a lie. Many gospels are being peddled in our world today, just as they were in Peter's day. The so-called Prosperity Gospel, Social Justice Gospel, and the Gay Gospel are all contemporary perversions of the good news of Jesus Christ.

First Corinthians 15:1, 3–4 states that the gospel is the death, burial, and resurrection of Jesus Christ according to Scripture. Anything added to the true message is a false gospel.

Advertisements of products that sound too good to be true are exactly that, too good to be true. False teachers expect to make a profit on God's Word (v. 3). They give a sales pitch to the spiritually gullible, planning to cash in on falsehood. The apostle Paul "renounced the things hidden because of shame, not walking in craftiness or adulterating the word of God" (2 Cor. 4:2).

According to contemporary culture, tolerance trumps all other religions. Absolute truth from God's Word is cast aside for political correctness. Such tolerance can be deadly! Why not tolerate a little strychnine in your coffee? Why not tolerate a little rattlesnake in the baby's crib? Why not tolerate a little fire on your clothing? The absurdity of tolerance in most cases illustrates that we must never deviate from the truth.

Punishment of Falsehood
2 Peter 2:3b–9

Most of the time it seems as if error goes unchecked. One day those who have intentionally distributed falsehood will be quiet and listen. Judgment is coming!

Three examples of God's judgment are used in these verses (vv. 3–8). An angelic rebellion took place before time began. It started with Lucifer, God's light bearer (see Isa. 14). One-third of the angels followed Lucifer in the rebellion against God (see Rev. 12:4). God's judgment was swift. These angels are now awaiting the final judgment.

In Noah's time the world was destroyed by a worldwide flood. Humankind had ventured so far away from God that it was necessary to remove everyone who rejected Him.

Sodom and Gomorrah experienced a tremendous outpouring of God's wrath. The account in Genesis 19 leaves no doubt that God's holiness will be vindicated.

Thankfully, God is a God of grace. Noah and Lot were spared from punishment. These exceptions tell us of the grace of God in the midst of His righteous judgment. All of us deserve punishment for our sins. Jesus paid the debt we could not pay. He is the expression of grace.

Sometimes we wonder why evildoers seemingly get away with defiance of God's grace. Those who never come under God's grace will suffer judgment either here or in the hereafter (1 Tim. 5:24). God is keeping the books.

Practice of Falsehood
2 Peter 2:10–19

Purveyors of falsehood exhibit certain characteristics. These ungodly traits are listed by Jude in verses 12 and 13. The activities they engage in come back on them. Heretics use certain tools in their craft. These tools are turned on them too.

Self-willed (2:10)

The Greek words *autos* (self) and *hadon* (pleasing) are the ingredients that incite rebellion against spiritual authority. Translated "self-willed" in the NASB, the word captures the essence of the false teacher. He exists for himself. He cares nothing for others. Life is all about his own satisfaction.

Unspiritual (2:11–14a)

False teachers are like animals that fail to sense spiritual reality. Their speech betrays their lack of respect for heavenly authority. The lies that destroy others devastate them as well. Sensual desires captivate their attention. Spiritual error is often revealed in fleshly sins. Open partying and adulterous activities expose the wayward heart.

Avarice (2:14b–16)

Balaam was willing to curse the people of God for a price (see Num. 22–24). People who sell out for monetary gain are accursed. At the beginning of their adulthood, these false teachers brought condemnation on themselves because of a desire for temporary possessions that superseded everything else.

Empty Promises (2:17–19)

Appealing to the bases of human nature, false teachers are able to gain a following. The weak and vulnerable are led away from the truth. The deceivers are empty with all promise but no delivery (see Prov. 25:14). Promising freedom, they can only produce slavery. The deceivers become slaves themselves. Surreptitious falsehood is the incipient seed of destruction.

Proof of Falsehood
2 Peter 2:20–22

Some would say these false teachers were saved and then became lost again. You cannot be saved today and lost tomorrow. These verses do not teach falling from grace. What the verses deal with is the evidence of salvation. True believers will continue in the truth. The end will be worse for those who hear the truth and twist it instead of receiving it. Deceivers will be worse off than if they had never known the truth.

Returning to a former lifestyle does not always indicate that a person is not a believer. However, repercussions are in store for those who are saved and disobey. The examples used by Peter show the false teachers never had a different nature. The repulsive example of a dog returning to its vomit clearly indicates that a dog is still a dog. The pig desiring to wallow in the mud has not become a sheep. For change to take place, a person must have a new nature (see 2 Pet. 1:4). For the desire for sin to be changed, a person must become a new creation. Paul wrote, "Therefore if anyone is in Christ, he _is_ a new creature; the old things passed away; behold, new things have come" (2 Cor. 5:17).

Peter was concerned about new believers. Just before Peter left for heaven, he wanted to warn them about deceivers. In almost two thousand years little has changed in this regard. We still need to be watchful at all times for those who would corrupt our faith by appealing to our base nature.

When will we be able to let down our guard? Spiritual warfare will end when we stand before Jesus. As long as the devil seeks to mislead those who would follow Christ, we must deal with his deception. Satan's main strategy in defeating believers is to deceive them (see 2 Cor. 11:3, 13–14). Many of the false teachers are deceived themselves. Peddlers of poison, heretics lead the unlearned and unspiritual to a path of destruction.

Be faithful to the truths of the Word of God. When a person proves to be a false teacher, after trying to bring him to the truth, if he does not return, then leave him alone (see Titus 3:10–11).

It has been said that one's orthodoxy is someone else's heresy. But the basic doctrines of the Christian faith cannot be compromised. The Southern Baptist Convention struggled to reestablish biblical fidelity in their seminaries and ministries. A movement known as the Conservative Resurgence began in 1979. By 1995 virtually all who were teaching doctrines contrary to adopted doctrinal statements were gone from leadership. Without clearly defined parameters of cooperation, it is impossible to assure biblical fidelity. What we believe about the Word of God has eternal consequences.

For Memory and Meditation
"Therefore if anyone is in Christ, he is a new creature; the old things passed away; behold, new things have come." 2 Corinthians 5:17

Chapter 11
Final Days That Are Challenging
Focal Text: 2 Peter 3:1–18

The first century was a time of cultural challenge for believers in Christ. Unusual events shook the relative calm of the Pax Romana. Christians faced persecution. False teachers invaded the church. Some thought Jesus was obligated to come back on their timetable. The apostle Peter addressed the issues of his time. He called for authentic Christianity. Peter believed that he was living in the last days. If he was living in the last days, we are in the last ticks of the clock. And still the times we live in call for authentic Christianity.

Recently I watched a great athlete in his prime announce his retirement. Injuries to his body had taken a toll. He could not continue with his career. All athletes come to that moment. The body cannot stand punishment year after year. It is sad but inevitable that an end comes to life itself. But, as believers in the Lord Jesus Christ, we have an assuring hope of eternal life with Him.

God is about to bring the curtain down on all of creation. It is not far away. The conclusion of life as we know it is the next item on God's agenda. Peter was leaving the new Christians with a word about the finality of all things. During persecution, discouragement, and even death, the expectation of Jesus's return was their strength. Psalm 46:1 assures us: "God is our refuge and strength, a very present help in trouble." We have encouraging words for difficult days.

The false teachers were denying Jesus's return. They refused to acknowledge a future judgment. Peter went directly to the issues. He said emphatically that Jesus will return. His promise is true. While we remain in this world, we are to be encouraged to respond to the challenges we face. In order to do so we must act upon Peter's counsel. Acting upon Peter's directives, we can be faithful in trying times.

Command of the Scriptures
2 Peter 3:1–2, 15–17

Peter recognized that his writing was equal in authority to the writings of the Old Testament. Peter called Paul's writings Scripture. Peter wanted his readers to rely on God's Word in times of challenge.

Authority (3:1–2)

Peter equates the Old Testament, the words of Jesus, and the writings of the apostles as authoritative. Peter echoes the apostle Paul from 2 Timothy 3:16: "All Scripture is inspired by God and profitable for teaching, for reproof, for correction, for training in righteousness."

Inspiration (3:15–16)

Peter did not mince words when he ascribed a supernatural origin to Paul's writings. Even though both Peter and Paul were writing letters to Christ followers in the first century, their words speak truth into our lives today; for the writings of both Peter said Paul were inspired in the same way as the Old Testament Scriptures. Only a spiritual mind can comprehend God's spiritual truth (see 1 Cor. 2:14).

Infallibility (3:17)

The Word of God will always lead to truth. Knowing the Scriptures will enable you to refute false teachers. And the more time you spend in God's Word and the more familiar you become with its teachings and the more you commit its words to memory, the better equipped you become to remain true to authentic Christianity. By God's Word you can have clear discernment to determine truth and what is not. Memorizing God's Word enables you to have a resource at your fingertips. We actually never gain command of the Scriptures; instead the Scriptures have command of us. Psalm 119 offers treasures of truth about God's Word. Verse 11 says, "Your word I have treasured in my heart, that I may not sin against You."

Confront the Scoffers
2 Peter 3:3-8, 16

"Scoffers" or "mockers" is translated from the Greek word *empaiktes*. The word gives a picture of people who turn their noses up at the truth. They are convinced they are better and know more than God and His Word. Proverbs 3:5–6 says, "Trust in the LORD WITH ALL YOUR HEART and do not lean on your own understanding. In all your ways acknowledge Him, and He will make your paths straight."

They Mock His Perfect character (3:3)

By living according to their own desires, the mockers defied a holy God. God is perfect in His character. He is sinless. He says in order for us to reflect Him, we are to pursue holiness (see 1 Pet. 1:16). Instead the mockers immersed themselves in sin.

They Mock His Promised Coming (3:4a)

Bible believers differ widely about the program of Jesus's return. The details may be debated. What cannot be equivocated is the reality of the event. The mockers jeered at the return of the Lord. Jesus promised He would come back (see Acts 1:11). Without a thought of the imminent return of Jesus, mockers were free to carry out their lustful desires. The expectation of His return should be ever present with the believer (see Titus 2:13). Jesus is coming again!

They Mock His Providential Control (3:4b–6)

Were the mockers actually denying the flood of Noah's day? They said all things continued as they were from the beginning of creation. Peter pointed out that the earth and its inhabitants had experienced cataclysmic change. Whatever transpires on this earth is under the watchful eye of a sovereign God. Romans 11:33–34 assures us that God is in control: "Oh, the depth of the riches both of the wisdom and knowledge of God! How unsearchable are His judgments and unfathomable His ways! For who has known the mind of the Lord, or who became His counselor?"

They Mock His Planned Consummation (3:7–8)

Judgment seems nonexistent for the mockers in the world today—just as it appeared to believers Peter addressed in the first century. They see no reckoning day. As God was in control on the first day, He will be in control on the last day. If God spoke the worlds into existence, then He can definitely bring about the end of time at His decree. When God ends all things, it will be by design and with a purpose. He has a plan. He will carry His plan at His pleasure, Psalm 115:3 tells us, "But our God is in the heavens; He does whatever He pleases."

Scoffers believe in themselves. Intellect, will, and self become the gods in the scoffers' belief system. Secular humanism and pseudo-intellectualism are a mockery to God and produce death.

In the late twentieth century so-called scholars gathered for a "Jesus Seminar" to determine if the sayings in the Gospels were actually uttered by Jesus. They came to the conclusion that little in the Gospel writings was actually from the lips of Jesus. Shortly after the turn of the twenty-first century, a follow-up study, "The Jesus Project," was launched to prove that the historical Jesus never existed. Instead they came to the conclusion that too many who were involved in the project had a bias of belief. R. Joseph Hoffmann wrote in "Threnody: Rethinking the Thinking behind the Jesus Project," "No quantum of material discovered since the 1940's, in the absence of canonical material, would support the existence of an historical founder. . . . No material regarded as canonical and no church doctrine built upon it in the history of the church would cause us to deny it. Whether the New Testament runs from Christ to Jesus or Jesus to Christ is not a question we can answer."

When belief in the inerrancy of Scripture is jettisoned, it will not be long until one doctrine after the other falls like dominos.

Commend God's Salvation
2 Peter 3:9

Peter preached the good news. God's part in the salvation process was reaffirmed. Peter honored God's grace by stating that God's promises would be fulfilled.

God offers salvation to all who come to Him. John wrote, "All that the Father gives Me will come to Me, and the one who comes to Me I will certainly not cast out" (John 6:37). God ordains the means of the salvation process. Sharing Jesus is our part to accomplish the biblical mandate. Paul wrote to the church in Rome: "How then will they call on Him in whom they have not believed? How will they believe in Him whom they have not heard? And how will they hear without a preacher?" (Rom. 10:14). Sharing the good news of redemption through Jesus Christ must become the priority in our lives. We are not commanded to make our culture Christian. We are commanded to present the gospel to everyone. Jesus last command was for His followers to go into all the world and make disciples. "Go therefore and make disciples of all the nations, baptizing them in the name of the Father and the Son and the Holy Spirit, teaching them to observe all that I commanded you; and lo, I am with you always, even to the end of the age." This is the only way to make a difference in people's lives. Even false teachers can repent and be saved.

Celebrate a Sovereign God
2 Peter 3:10, 12–13

The Scriptures use different terms for end-time events. "The day of the Lord" may refer to the end of time or to some other event prior to it. As I said earlier, the events surrounding Jesus's return are debatable. What we can be sure of is that He is coming again.

Reality of Judgment (3:10, 12)

Peter was concerned about false teachers eroding the faith of baby Christians. Heretics refused to recognize accountability to anyone. This gave them license to sin. Peter reinforced the fact that God would bring a final judgment on this world.

Rejoicing in Jesus' Presence (3:13)

Heaven is a place of perfection (see Rev. 21). When confronted by mockers, discouraged by circumstance, or plagued by our failings, there is promise of relief. Heaven is real. It is imperative for us to look for the return of our Lord Jesus. Are you longing for Him? There is no greater strength than when we are anticipating His soon return.

Conform to the Savior's Image
2 Peter 3:11, 14, 17–18

Holiness was not an option in the first century. Many believers were called upon to seal their testimonies with their lives. Persecution emboldens followers of Jesus to be witnesses.

Lifestyle (3:11)

When we look for the return of the Lord, we should be motivated to live more godly lives. The apostle wrote, "And everyone who has this hope fixed on Him purifies himself, just as He is pure" (1 John 3:3). When we look up, He will clean us up. Paul wrote to the church at Corinth, "Therefore, having these promises, beloved, let us cleanse ourselves from all defilement of flesh and spirit, perfecting holiness in the fear of God" (2 Cor. 7:1). God has called us to be different from the world system. We are to be a holy people in an unholy world.

Love (3:14)

Living within sight of the return of the Lord should cause us to love one another as we see the day approaching. The birthmark of every Christian is love. Jesus taught the Twelve, "By this all men will know that you are My disciples, if you have love for one another" (John 13:35). These words are still true for us today—Christians in harmony picture a future state when we will live without strife.

Loyalty (3:17–18)

Some who profess eternal life do not possess eternal life. The false teachers lead true believers away from growing in Christ. We are challenged to continue to mature in Christ. Our spiritual growth continues until we leave this life.

All that we are and ever accomplish is to the glory of God! This sums up our purpose on this earth.

Conclusion

Second Peter is a small letter to all believers. The early church had already been infiltrated by deceivers. Doctrinal departures were threatening the advancement of the gospel. Peter was concerned that after his death the new believers might be carried off into false teaching denying the return of Jesus and a final judgment. In writing his farewell, knowing his death was likely soon, Peter addressed these issues. He echoed the apostle Paul's sentiments to stay faithful until Jesus comes. Peter made clear that we are to look for Jesus and live for Him every day. Peter spoke encouraging words for difficult days. Those words remain to speak to us today.

For Memory and Meditation

"The Lord is not slow about His promise, as some count slowness, but is patient toward you, not wishing for any to perish but for all to come to repentance." 2 Peter 3:9

Introduction to Jude

Jude was writing twenty plus years after Jesus's ascension in the mid-60s AD. Several men named James are mentioned in the New Testament. James, the disciple of Jesus who became leader of the Jerusalem church, had already been martyred (see Acts 12:2). Many conservative scholars say that the James mentioned in verse 1 was the half brother of Jesus and Jude's brother. Perhaps Jude was too humble to mention that he was Jesus's half brother (see Matt. 13:55).

Jude intended to write about the gospel. He starts his letter with a common but joyful salutation. He moved quickly to warn believers of false teachers. Jude used Old Testament accounts, extrabiblical examples, and descriptions of ungodly behavior. The false teachers were subverting God's Word, especially the gospel. Errant belief produces evil behavior. Jude said these unrepentant false teachers would eventually face judgment. The letter ends with a challenge to believers, then is capped with a doxology of praise.

My wife and I have three children. Our girls were much older when our son was born. A boy is different in many ways, especially his toys. Nathan had a construction site set with buttons that activated recordings. One night my wife got up to check on him. She stepped on the construction site. A warning blared out, "Caution." You can imagine the truth in that statement.

Jude is telling the church, "Caution." Danger is lurking. False teachers can cause damage to the individual believer as well as the church as a whole. We have a pointed warning about false teachers.

Chapter 12
Warnings to the Ungodly
Focal Text: Jude 1–14

Person of the Letter
Jude 1–2

We have already looked at the authorship of the letter. Liberals theorize that Jude was written by an imposter. They would say that at best this little book was written by a well-meaning person who used the pseudonym Jude. While arguments can be made for another author, we have no reason to reject that Jude, Jesus's half brother, wrote the letter. The authority of the Holy Spirit is evident in the words of this letter.

Jude is addressing believers in Christ. His audience is the redeemed of the church. He may have been writing to a particular church, but the letter could also have been circulated among the early churches. He reassures the saved of their security in Christ.

A common but joyful salutation is offered to the believers. Jude expresses a prayer of blessing for the recipients of his letter.

Purpose of the Letter
Jude 3–4

Jude intended to write about the gospel. The gospel is "that Christ died for our sins according to the Scriptures, and that He was buried, and that He was raised on the third day according to the Scriptures" (1 Cor. 15:3–4). Jude desired to converse about the joyous gift of eternal life in Christ. Jude changed his theme at the beginning of the letter. He issues a call to believers to contend for the faith against false teachers. "The faith" is different from "faith." "The faith" is a system of doctrine and truth as expressed in God's Word.

Danger was already in the church. False teachers had weaseled their way into a position of influence. Unsaved men sought to undermine the authority of God's Word and the person of Jesus Christ.

Our system of doctrine must come from the Bible. The Bible is the true measure of what we believe. Years ago when I first attended college, I was confronted with professors who denied the virgin birth, bodily resurrection, and exclusivity of salvation in Jesus Christ. I had to decide whether I would follow the teaching of recognized theologians or trust in the veracity of the Word of God. My life and ministry have been defined by that decision I made long ago. I chose to take the Scriptures as totally true and trustworthy. Sometimes we must defend the truth. We must do it kindly but without wavering.

Prophesy in the Letter
Jude 5–19

Verses 5–19 are one paragraph in the original language. Jude used Old Testament accounts, extrabiblical examples, and descriptions of the ungodly. False teachers were subverting God's Word, especially the gospel. Errant belief produces evil behavior. Jude said these unrepentant false teachers would eventually face judgment.

Second Peter 2 and Jude have much in common. Some propose that one copied from the other, a type of spiritual plagiarism. It is possible that Peter read Jude's letter. With false teachers springing up in the church, it would be more likely that the two appeals to avoid doctrinal error were written separately.

Examples and Characteristics (vv. 5–11)

Israel, angels, Sodom, Michael, Cain, Balaam, and Korah are cited as departures from the truth. Common characteristics of deceivers are to defile, defy, denigrate (v. 8).

Old Testament Examples (vv. 5–7)

Israel lost a generation in the wilderness due to unbelief. They did not enter into God's promise. They fell short in unbelief. First John 5:16 offers a warning to Christians about a sin unto death: "If you see any brother or sister commit a sin that does not lead to death, you should pray and God will give them life. I refer to those whose sin does not lead to death. There is a sin that leads to death. I am not saying that you should pray about that." A believer can commit a certain sin or sin in a certain way so many times that his disobedience would cost his life. God is a God of love. He is a God of holiness too. Unbelief or disobedience can bring the judgment of God.

Angels rebelled against God when they followed Lucifer. They fell from heaven never to be reclaimed. They lost their place because they wanted a higher position. There is no redemption for angels. Jesus died for people. This example could not be about people losing their salvation. The angels never were saved. The rebellious angels were expelled from the presence of God. The angels mentioned in this verse are consigned to "Tartarus," another compartment of hell (see 2 Pet. 2:4). This is a unique word used to describe a particular place of confinement until their final judgment.

Sodom and Gomorrah and Noah's flood were verified by the Lord Jesus as recorded in Luke 17:28–30. Projecting the ages of Noah's sons by the longevity of life in Genesis, it is possible that Noah's sons were alive at the time of God's judgment on Sodom and Gomorrah. If they were alive, they witnessed another—although not universal—judgment of God. People think judgment will not come. Sinful behavior is accelerated because judgment seems to be delayed. Ecclesiastes 8:11 explains why people proceed in sin with a flawed understanding of God's judgment: "When the sentence for a crime is not quickly carried out, people's hearts are filled with schemes to do wrong."

Characteristics of Apostates (vv. 8–10)

The false teachers were fantasizing about sinful pleasures—much like pornography has gripped so many today. Fantasizing pushed the false teachers to reject God's authority. The word "defile" means "to dye" or "to stain." Rejecting authority was a conscious sin, a sin of the mind. Once allowed to captivate the mind, the natural result is physical sin.

Claiming certain verses of Scriptures as obligating God to act is the height of arrogance. Even Michael, the archangel, did not order Satan around. Instead Michael depended on the power of God.

Ungodly Men (v. 11)

Three apostates are listed as exhibit one in the case Jude is prosecuting against false teachers. Cain took the wrong approach to come into God's presence. He pursued a bloodless avenue. Those in error teach that you can have Christ without the cross and redemption without the blood. Balaam had the wrong affection. His desire was all about money. Prosperity gospel preachers present a false appeal by replacing a longing for God with a pursuit for money. Korah had the wrong attitude. His attack of Moses was motivated by pride wanting the power over the people. Korah cared nothing about the proclamation of God's Word.

Nature's Pictures of Deception (vv. 12–13)

A hidden reef could sink a ship. These men put obstacles in people's lives that would cause damage. Whether fellowship meals or the Lord's Supper, deceivers continually think only of themselves. They are clouds promising refreshment, but they bring no rain. Trees without fruit are often dead on the inside. The only curse uttered from Jesus's lips was on a tree that produced no fruit (see Matt. 21:18–22). Waves produce foam and deposit dirt. False teachers create unsavory conditions by their doctrines. They are like shooting stars. A flash in the sky is all they amount to. They have no lasting illumination.

Enoch's Prediction (vv. 14–15)

Jude quoted an extrabiblical document. It does not mean the quote came from some lost book of the Bible. Other noninspired references are incorporated in the Word of God. Oral tradition in the Jewish community may have transmitted the truth of Enoch's prophecy. Regardless, we can be confident that Enoch said it and that it will come true. Jesus is coming again!

Jude used the past tense in the word "came" to announce the Lord Jesus's return. It is as sure as if it had already happened. It will take place. The first time Jesus came, He came with a cross to bear. The next time Jesus comes, He will have a crown to wear. He was the Lamb of God in His first advent.

In His second advent He will be the Lion of Judah. Justice is coming!

Four times the word "ungodly" is used in verse 15. Antinomianism is a disregard for God's laws. The Greek word for "ungodly" is *asebeo*, which carries the same disregard against God's person. Ungodliness in this context is more personal toward God.

Characteristics of Apostates (vv. 16–19)

Three evident characteristics are seen in these verses. Apostates use their mouths to deceive. They make their appeal with their lips (v. 16). They will eventually expose their own sensual sins. They express their false doctrine through their lives (vv. 17–18). Finally, Jude said they are not believers, for they do not possess the Holy Spirit. The apostates are lost (v. 19).

Murmurers cause problems in the church by complaining about trivial matters. Troublemakers find fault in almost everything. They are complainers. "Finding fault" is translated from a unique Greek word found nowhere else in the New Testament. An uncommon word is used for a common practice. Walking after their lusts is the eventual outcome of rejecting God and His Word. Apostates use words to deceive, thereby creating trouble in the church. The apostates never had the indwelling Spirit of God (see Acts 8:21).

Believers must test all teaching by the Word of God. Only the Bible can be the perfect gauge to measure truth. The sad end of the false teacher is an eternity away from God.

Most people have heard of Billy Graham, but few have heard of Charles Templeton. After World War II they were both prominent evangelists. They traveled together during preaching crusades. After many successful ministries Templeton began to doubt the Genesis account of creation. He had a conversation with Graham. He told Graham it was intellectual suicide to believe the Bible. Templeton decided to attend Princeton where his confidence in God's Word was further eroded. Eventually Templeton became an agnostic. His last book is entitled *Farewell to God*.

How can a person so gifted turn out to be a fraud? Many have intellectual assent to the truth but never have a personal relationship with Jesus. Apostates are in the church. It is up to the believer to test all teaching by the Word of God.

Practicality of the Letter
Jude 20–25

Jude ends his letter with encouragement for believers capped with a doxology of praise. When all seems bleak, God sends a ray of sunshine. Jude turns to the practical application. With all that is going on around the church in culture and what happens in the church, believers can still be encouraged.

Living Out the Faith in a Hostile Place (vv. 20–23)

Just before concluding the letter, Jude uses four participles to encourage action in contending for the faith. These participles challenge us to action. There are four simple activities that can help us contend for the faith.

Building—This is a construction analogy. The foundation and the superstructure must be solid. A "holy" faith is different from other belief. It is objective and experiential (see 2 Tim. 2:15; 3:15). We are not asked to have blind faith. We are to have reasonable faith. God's Word makes sense. We build our system of beliefs on the infallible authority of God's Word.

Praying—Tongue speaking is not mentioned in relation to praying in the Holy Spirit. Of the six words used in the New Testament for *prayer*, this is the most common. It means to have regular communion with God. We need the empowerment of the Spirit to pray. We are instructed by the Holy Spirit about how to pray. When we don't know what to pray, the Holy Spirit intercedes for us.

This is different from the religious exercises of the false teachers. God's Spirit will never direct us contrary to His Word. Prayer changes us more than it changes circumstances. We cannot manipulate God. We place ourselves under the Spirit's leadership.

Keeping—Keeping in the love of God means we are in a place where God can best bless us. Being in God's love is more about His love for us than our love for Him. In Luke 15 the Father never stopped loving the prodigal son even when the son was outside the Father's protection and provision. The son was still loved. He was simply outside of the protection and provision of the father.

This admonition is not about keeping ourselves saved. It is about being in a right position of fellowship with the Father.

Looking—Translated in the NASB as "waiting anxiously," the thought is for us to have an expectant longing for Jesus's return. When Jesus returns, we will experience the fulfillment of God's promises.

Our Witness (vv. 22–23)

There is a distinction between two types of individuals who need spiritual assistance. Winning people to Christ as well as retrieving people from false doctrine includes compassion. "Mercy" is a godly pity for those who have gone astray. We are to have patience with those who doubt. For others we must be willing to take extraordinary action. Getting someone from a burning building requires dramatic effort. Intervention in the face of danger is necessary.

Compassion or confrontation requires caution in the way you carry out your witness. We try to correct those in error without being drawn away ourselves.

When I was a young preacher, there was a bold witness known as the Chaplain of Bourbon Street. He did his ministry in the middle of the debauchery in the New Orleans French Quarter. Many people came to Christ through his courageous witness. Sadly he let his guard down. He lost his testimony and ministry by falling into the very sins he was trying to get people delivered from. Today he publicly regrets his failing. He warns others to be careful if they are involved in intervention gospel ministry.

God Is Able (vv. 24–25)

He is able to provide security for our salvation. For the true believer there will be no apostasy. We may stumble along in life, but we will be lifted up by our Heavenly Father. An earthly father delights in the steps of his child. The father holds the child's hand until it is time to let the child walk. When the child falls, the father picks her up again. He restores us, making us usable for His glory. We may fail Him, but He will never fail us.

In the last days God will complete His saving work. We go from the possibility of stumbling to being perfected in His presence. The appearance of the church at the coming of Christ will be without blemish. The Greek word *amemitos* means "without any shortcoming." The word was used to describe an animal worthy of sacrifice in worship. We are not sinless this side of heaven, but God is making us like Jesus! We are being conformed into His image.

Nothing satisfies like Jesus. When we are in the presence of His glory, we will have exceeding joy. Fame, fortune, or even family cannot satisfy the longing in our souls. Only Jesus can fill the void. Our strength for living comes from the

Lord (see Neh. 8:10). Happiness depends on circumstances. Joy comes from within.

God is our Savior. Some translations have the words "to the only wise God." While both are true, there is no question the God spoken of is Jesus.

There is no one like our God. First Chronicles 29:11 tells of the awesomeness of our God: "Yours, O Lord, is the greatness and the power and the glory and the victory and the majesty, indeed everything that is in the heavens and the earth; Yours is the dominion, O Lord, and You exalt Yourself as head over all." The description contained in the crescendo of praise goes beyond our ability to comprehend. Many of God's attributes are described. His glory is a divine radiance of the One worthy of worship. His Majesty speaks of His transcendence. His dominion expresses His sovereignty. His power is evident in the authority He possesses. All of these descriptions of our God have always been true, are true, and will forever be true.

We join with Jude in saying "amen" to all that has gone before in this letter, especially this closing doxology about God. The chorus of the redeemed say, "Let it be."

When you get discouraged, remember, we have a God who is able! He is able to provide salvation, strength, and security.

For Memory and Meditation
"But you, beloved, building yourselves up on your most holy faith, praying in the Holy Spirit, keep yourselves in the love of

God, waiting anxiously for the mercy of our Lord Jesus Christ to eternal life." Jude 20–21